HOW MARKET WORKS IN INDIA

ARIB UMAR

ISBN 979-888530507-5

For Beginner

Contents

Prologue

How people survive? In market.
How it works? How you work?
Let's begin

CHAPTER ONE

Introduction

1. Introduction

Did anyone break a mentality of Indian people? About teens.

In other countries every teen learn about crypto or stocks in his high school. But India 'no'. In our country everyone things that the government job is enough for life but the reality is different no one understand this. Parents does not allow his child to learn about this. They think this is a kind of bad games where everyone lose his money and get addicted toward it.

But, why?

Indian parents has a fixed mentality that his child only get succeed whenever he got a government job. But they don't understand the life has much this that they do not know about.

We have to change this thing let me tell you a interesting story about warren buffet At **11 years old** he made his first investment, buying three shares of Cities Service Preferred at $38 per share. The stock quickly dropped to only $27, but Buffett held on tenaciously until it reached $40.

Then he became richest person in the world.

Everyone knows warren buffet as king of market but no one knows about our existence.

Did you know why?

Because of our way of education. We learn what we are taught we don't feel any force from our side.

So encourage everyone who want to learn.

Let's back to our first question 'Did anyone of break a mentality Indian people?'

No, no one wants you to go ahead but there is twist in life not everyone is same some people is very helpful they teach us how to go up. In my life I have seen many people that help me a lot and push me to go ahead. 'Thanks' and I am very thankful to him.

'Hope you understand'

CHAPTER TWO

How to start

The very first question came to our mind is ‘how to start’

Before we start let me tell you a very interesting story ‘in a village there is a man who believe in god and do worship every day. Every time he say to god please god please make me winner of lottery. this continue many years one day he is near to die he say to god ‘ now I am not able to believe in you because I was worship everyday but you does not give me result that I wanted after this god says politely ’child I am ready here to give you result but you does not buy any ticket so how I make you winner'.

Know you know why I am telling you to start because start is the first step toward the success. Let’s back to point

How to enroll in share market how to buy or how to sell. Let me explain.

What share market is?

Basically, we say that this is a place where we can buy or sell share.

Now the question came to our mind is

What is share?

Basically, Shares are units of equity ownership in a corporation. For some companies, shares exist as a financial asset providing for an equal distribution of any residual profits, if any are declared, in the form of dividends.

Shareholders of a stock that pays no dividends do not participate in a distribution of profits. Instead, they anticipate participating in the growth of the stock price as company profits increase.

Shares represent equity stock in a firm, with the two main types of shares being common shares and preferred shares. As a result, "shares" and "stock" are commonly used interchangeably.

Let me explain you with an example

'You have an empty plot of area 1200 sq. ft. You have to need some money so you say everyone to plant a tree on your plot then take 2$ for every tree now 100 tree are planted but 30 people cut his tree when he is not too big and sell them for 4$ they make profit of 2$ but after some time 70 tree became big they sell on 10$ each they make profit of 8$ on each tree '

Know I hope you understand about what is share.

Know we talk about how to but any company share.

You know that our bank are under RBI but we cannot open our account under RBI we use some brokers or external banks that work for us under RBI.

Similarly, all this type of transaction is control by SEBI "The Securities and Exchange Board of India "

There are two much broker that do this work for you.

In India there are two way to buy stock.

NSE "national stock exchange" or

BSE "Bombay Stock Exchange"

There is many way you can use to buy the stocks in India you go through their official website or you use broker in-between them.

We call them stock exchange. Let me explain

What Is a Stock Exchange?

Stock exchanges are secondary markets where existing shareholders can transact with potential buyers. It is important to understand that the corporations listed on stock markets do not buy and sell their own shares on a regular basis. Companies may engage in stock buybacks or issue new shares but these are not day-to-day operations and often occur outside of the framework of an exchange.

So when you buy a share of stock on the stock market, you are not buying it from the company, you are buying it from some other existing shareholder. Likewise, when you sell your shares, you do not sell them back to the company—rather you sell them to some other investor.

History of Stock Exchanges

The first stock markets appeared in Europe in the 16th and 17th centuries, mainly in port cities or trading hubs such as Antwerp, Amsterdam, and London.[3] These early stock exchanges, however, were more akin to bond exchanges as the small number of companies did not issue equity. In fact, most early corporations were considered semi-public organizations since they had to be chartered by their government in order to conduct business.

In the late 18th century, stock markets began appearing in America, notably the New York Stock Exchange (NYSE), which allowed for equity shares to trade. The honour of the first stock exchange in America goes to the Philadelphia Stock Exchange (PHLX), which still exists today.[4] The NYSE was founded in 1792 with the signing of the Buttonwood Agreement by 24 New York City stockbrokers and merchants. Prior to this official incorporation, traders and brokers would meet unofficially under a buttonwood tree on Wall Street to buy and sell shares.[5]

The advent of modern stock markets ushered in an age of regulation and professionalization that now ensures buyers and sellers of shares can trust that their transactions will go through at fair prices and within a reasonable period of time. Today, there are many stock exchanges in the U.S. and throughout the world, many of which are linked together electronically. This in turn means markets are more efficient and more liquid.

Example 1 how broker work between us.

Now learn with this image and then we will begin new chaplet.

CHAPTER THREE

Greed and Fear

The fear and greed index is **a tool used by some investors to gauge the market**. It is based on the premise that excessive fear can result in stocks trading well below their intrinsic values while, at the same time, unbridled greed can result in stocks being bid up far above what they should be worth.

Fear create panic and panic creates supply in the market place.

Greed produces exuberance give rise to demand. Now the new question came to our mind is how demand and supply works in market

In a Competitive Market , the unit price for a particular good will vary until it settle at a point where quantity demanded by consumers (at current price) will equal the quantity supplied by producers (at current price),resulting in an Economic Equilibrium for price and quantity.

Let me share you a story of greed

I met with my brother he told me about his friend who is illiterate he told me that his grandfather working in a company is giving him a little amount of company share with his salary but after the death of his grandfather . the company launched his IPO and my brothers friend has worth 1 lakh rupees share of this company now his friend is in tension how to withdraw money from this they try to much for making a trading account but he failed after few days he successfully open a demat account with a offer of refer and earn know he star t forcing people in greed of earning few money but his friend is illiterate he does not know about annual maintenance charge he opened many people account without saying about its annual maintenance charge when everyone knows about his annual maintenance charge they are started saying them that they do fraud to us.

So keep distance from this type of people do what you understand.

The fear and greed index is **a tool used by some investors to gauge the market.** It is based on the premise that excessive fear can result in stocks trading well below their intrinsic values while, at the same time, unbridled greed can result in stocks being bid up far above what they should be worth.

Fear create panic and panic creates supply in the market place.

Greed produces exuberance give rise to demand. Now the new question came to our mind is how demand and supply works in market

In a Competitive Market , the unit price for a particular good will vary until it settle at a point where quantity demanded by consumers (at current price) will equal the quantity supplied by producers (at current price),resulting in an Economic Equilibrium for price and quantity.

Let me share you a story of greed

I met with my brother he told me about his friend who is illiterate he told me that his grandfather working in a company is giving him a little amount of company share with his salary but after the death of his grandfather . the company launched his IPO and my brothers friend has worth 1 lakh rupees share of this company now his friend is in tension how to withdraw money from this they try to much for making a trading account but he failed after few days he successfully open a demat account with a offer of refer and earn know he star t forcing people in greed of earning few money but his friend is illiterate he does not know about annual maintenance charge he opened many people account without saying about its annual maintenance charge when everyone knows about his annual maintenance charge they are started saying them that they do fraud to us.

So keep distance from this type of people do what you understand.

CHAPTER FOUR

Big Mistake

1. The fall of Yes Bank

On March 5, 2020, the Reserve Bank of India (RBI) imposed a 30-day moratorium on YES Bank, superseded the private-sector lender's board, and appointed Prashant Kumar, who was serving as chief financial officer and deputy managing director at State Bank of India (SBI), as an administrator. Under the terms of the moratorium, deposit withdrawals were capped at Rs 50,000 per person. The central bank proposed a reconstruction scheme under which SBI might take a maximum of 49% stake in the restructured capital of the bank. Analysts believed the new management of YES Bank, headed by former Deutsche Bank India head Ravneet Gill, who joined the bank in early 2019, could turn around the ship. Gill, however, has struggled to do so.

A brief history of YES Bank

YES Bank Ltd runs three units – YES Asset Management Services, YES Capital and YES Bank. Once the country's fifth-largest private lender by market capitalisation, YES Bank had been founded by Rana Kapoor and Ashok Kapoor in 2004. In the year 2005, the bank forayed into retail banking with the launch of International Gold and Silver debit card in partnership with MasterCard International. In June 2005, YES Bank came out with a public issue and its shares were listed on the stock exchanges. The bank was ranked number 1 bank in the Business Today-KPMG Best Banks Annual Survey 2008. YES Bank was the first institution globally to receive funding through IFC's Managed Co-Lending Portfolio Programme and the first Indian bank to raise loan under IFC's A/B loan facility. On September 2014, YES Bank announced it had received a ratings upgrade from credit rating agency ICRA and CARE for its various long-term debt programmes. On December 18, 2017, YES Bank made its entry in the 30-share S&P BSE Sensex. A few months later, YES Bank announced the listing of the bank's debut $600-million bond issue under its maiden $1 billion MTN programme on Global Securities Market (GSM) – India's first capital-raising platform for international investors in any currency located at the Gujarat International Finance Tec-City (GIFT City) IFSC.

In December 2017, the bank's branch network stood at 1,050 and its ATM network at 1,724.

What has led to a crisis at YES Bank?

The bank's loan book on March 31, 2014, was Rs 55,633 crore, and its deposits were Rs 74,192 crore. Since then, the loan book has grown to nearly four times as much, at Rs 2.25 trillion as on September 30, 2019. While deposit growth failed to keep pace and increased at less than three times to Rs 2.10 trillion. The bank's asset quality also worsened and it came under regulator RBI's scanner. YES Bank has a substantial exposure to several troubled borrowers, including the Anil Ambani-led Reliance group, DHFL and IL&FS. The tipping point came when one of the bank's independent directors Uttam Prakash Agarwal, resigned from the board in January 2020 citing governance issues.

Here are several reasons behind the crisis at the new-age private-sector bank

1. NPAs: YES Bank ran into trouble following the central bank's asset quality reviews in 2017 and 2018, which led to a sharp increase in its impaired loans ratio and uncovered significant governance lapses that led to a complete change of management. The bank subsequently struggled to address its capitalisation issues. YES Bank suffered a dramatic doubling in its gross NPAs between April and September 2019 to Rs 17,134 crore.

2. NBFC crisis: The crisis in India's shadow-banking space started with the unravelling of Infrastructure Leasing & Financial Services (IL&FS) and then extended to Dewan Housing Finance Limited (DHFL). YES Bank's total exposure to IL&FS and DHFL was 11.5 per cent as of September 2019. In April 2019, the bank had classified about Rs 10,000 crore of its exposures, representing 4.1 per cent of its total loans under watch list, as potential non-performing loans over the next 12 months.

3. Governance issue: YES Bank faced several governance issues that led to its decline. On January 10, independent director Uttam Prakash Agarwal quit citing deteriorating corporate governance standards and compliance failure at the lender. In 2018-19, the bank under-reported NPAs to the tune of Rs 3,277 crore, prompting RBI to dispatch R Gandhi, one of its former deputy governors, to the board of the bank. Rana Kapoor, who was instrumental in building YES Bank from scratch, was asked to step down as chief executive in January 2019.

4. Excessive withdrawals: YES Bank's financial condition dissuaded many depositors from keeping funds in the bank over a longer term. The bank showed a steady withdrawal of deposits, which burdened its balance sheet and added to its woes. The bank had a deposit book of Rs 2.09 trillion at the end of September 2019.

What action has RBI taken against YES Bank?

— RBI has taken over the YES Bank management

— The central has imposed a moratorium on the lender

— RBI announced a draft 'Scheme of Reconstruction' that entails SBI investing capital to acquire a 49% stake in the restructured private lender.

Why was a moratorium imposed on YES Bank?

The banking regulator, while recommending a moratorium, cited a steady decline in YES Bank's financial position, mainly due to the lender's inability to raise adequate capital to make provisions for potential non-performing assets. This failing resulted in downgrades by credit rating agencies, which in turn made capital raising even more difficult. This apart, there were serious lapses in corporate governance at the bank.

How does a moratorium work?

A moratorium is a temporary suspension of activity until future events warrant lifting of the suspension or related issues have been resolved.

In case of YES Bank, RBI has imposed a month-long moratorium which is scheduled to end on April 3.

Hence, a customer can withdraw a maximum of Rs 50,000 during this period from their savings or current or any other deposit accounts. In case a depositor has more than one deposit account with YES Bank, then the moratorium will apply cumulatively on all their accounts. There's a small relief to depositors in cases of emergencies. RBI has said that one could withdraw up to Rs 5 lakh for medical emergencies, higher education expenses, payments towards marriage, other ceremonies and "unavoidable emergencies".

What next for YES Bank?

The RBI has a draft reconstruction plan for YES Bank which proposes that depositors' funds would be protected. The employees would also have the same service conditions, including remuneration, at least for one year. However, in the case of key managerial personnel, the new board would be empowered to take a call.

The SBI, which has received a board approval to invest in YES Bank, will pick up to a 49% stake, according to the scheme, at a price that is not less than Rs 10 for each share having a face value of Rs 2.

SBI also cannot reduce its holding below 26% before the completion of three years from the date of infusion of the capital.

Who is Rana Kapoor and what's the case against him?

Rana Kapoor is a co-founder and former managing director & chief executive of YES Bank. Born in 1957 in Delhi, Kapoor started his professional journey as a junior banker in Bank of America's Barakhamba branch in New Delhi. He worked with BoA for 16 years. In 1998, Rana Kapoor joined his brother-in-law Ashok Kapur and Harkirat Singh to form Rabo India Finance. Kapur, Kapoor and Singh sold their equity in the venture in 2003 and got the licence to set up a private sector bank (YES Bank). Kapoor was well-networked in the corporate sector and he found his niche in companies that were finding it difficult to get financing from other existing lenders. In September 2018, he was asked to step down as the chairman of YES Bank and was replaced by Ravneet Gill.

CHAPTER FIVE

NSE LAWS

Laws for stock market

NATIONAL STOCK EXCHANGE OF INDIA LIMITED RULES

ARRANGEMENT OF CHAPTERS Chapter Description I. Board II. Executive Committee III. Trading Membership IV. Disciplinary Proceeding, Penalties Suspension and Expulsion I.BOARD (1) The Board of Directors (herein referred to as Board) of National Stock Exchange of India Limited, constituted in accordance with the provisions of the Articles of Association of the Company, may organize, maintain, control, manage, regulate and facilitate the operations of the Exchange and of securities transactions by trading members of the Exchange, subject to the provisions of the Securities Contracts (Regulation) Act, 1956 and Rules thereunder, Securities and Exchange Board of India Act, 1992 and any directives thereunder and the trading regulations which RBI may prescribe from time to time for money market instruments. (2) Directors of the National Stock Exchange of India Limited shall be appointed in accordance with the provisions of the Articles of Association of the Company as amended from time to time and in particular, provisions of Articles 108, 109, 110, 111, 112, 113, 114, 115 and 116 thereof. Any such appointment of Directors shall be considered as one being made under the provisions of these rules. (3) Subject to the provisions of the Securities Contracts (Regulation) Act, 1956 and Rules thereunder, the Securities and Exchange Board of India Act, 1992 and any directives thereunder and the trading regulations which RBI may prescribe from time to time for money market instruments, the Board is empowered to make Bye Laws, Rules and Regulations from time to time, for all or any matters relating to the conduct of business of the Exchange, the business and transactions of trading members between trading members inter-se as well as the business and transactions between trading members and persons who are not trading members, and to control, define and regulate all such transactions and dealings and to do such acts and things which are necessary for the purposes of the Exchange. (3A) The composition of the Board shall consist of the following categories namely Public Interest Directors, Shareholder Directors (including employee Directors) and Managing Director. (4) Without prejudice to the generality of the foregoing, the Board is empowered to make Regulations, subject to the provisions of the Securities Contracts (Regulation) Act, 1956 and Rules thereunder, the Securities and Exchange Board of India Act, 1992 and any directives thereunder and the trading regulations which RBI may prescribe from time to time for money market instruments, for all or any of the following matters: (a) Conditions for admission to membership of the Exchange; (b) Conditions for any arrangement with another stock exchange pursuant to the proviso to Section 13 of the Securities Contracts (Regulation) Act, 1956 and all matters relating thereto 1 (c) Conduct of business of the Exchange; (d) Conduct of trading members with regard to the business of the

Exchange; (e) Penalties for disobedience or contravention of the Rules, Bye Laws and Regulations of the Exchange or of general discipline of the Exchange, including expulsion or suspension of the trading members; (f) Declaration of any trading member as a defaulter or suspension or resignation or expulsion from trading membership of the Exchange and consequences thereof; (g) Conditions, levy for admission or subscription for admission or continuance of trading membership of the Exchange; (h) Charges payable by trading members for transactions in such securities as may be laid down from time to time; (i) Investigation of the financial condition, business conduct and dealings of the trading members; (j) Appointment of Committee or Committees for any purpose of the Exchange; (k) Such other matters in relation to the Exchange as may be prescribed under the provisions of the Articles of Association, Bye Laws or these Rules or as may be necessary or expedient for the organisation, maintenance, control, management, regulation and facilitation of the operations of the Exchange. (5) The Board is empowered to delegate, from time to time, to the Executive Committee(s) or to the Managing Director or to any person, such of the powers vested in it and upon such terms as they may think fit, to manage all or any of the affairs of the Exchange and from time to time, to revoke, withdraw, alter or vary all or any of such powers. (6) The Board may, from time to time, constitute one or more committees comprising of members of the Board or such others as the Board may in its discretion deem fit or necessary and delegate to such committees such powers as the Board may deem fit and the Board may from time to time revoke such delegation. The Committees constituted by the Board may inter alia include : (a) Admissions

Committee for admission of trading members of the Exchange; (b) Infrastructure Committee to recommend appropriate infrastructure and implement the same; (c) Systems Committee to recommend setting up of systems for carrying on the functioning of the Exchange and to implement and monitor the same; (d) Any other matter which the Board may think fit. 2 (7) The Board shall have the authority to issue directives from time to time to the Executive Committee or any other Committees or any other person or persons to whom any powers have been delegated by the Board. Such directives issued in exercise of this power, which may be of policy nature or may include directives to dispose off a particular matter or issue, shall be binding on the concerned Committee(s) or person(s). (8) Subject to the provisions of the Securities Contracts (Regulation) Act, 1956 and Rules thereunder, the Securities and Exchange Board of India Act, 1992 and any directives thereunder and the trading regulations which RBI may prescribe from time to time for money market instruments, the Board is empowered to vary, amend, repeal or add to Bye Laws, Rules and Regulations framed by it. (9) The Members of the Board and of such committees as may be identified by the Ethics Committee shall adhere to the Code of Conduct as may be prescribed by the Board or Ethics Committee from time to time. 3 II. EXECUTIVE COMMITTEE Constitution (1) One or more Executive Committee(s) shall be appointed by the Board for the purposes of managing the day to day affairs of the different trading segment(s). (2) Executive Committee(s) appointed by the Board shall consist of: (a) Managing Director of the Company, (b) [deleted] (c) Not more than four trading members as may be nominated by the Board as per Rules laid down in this regard, (d) Such individual persons of eminence in the field of finance, accounting, law or other discipline and to be known as 'public representatives' as may be nominated by the Board. (e) Four persons nominated in that behalf by the Board, to be known as 'other nominees', which may include two ex-officio senior officers of the Company. The maximum strength of the Executive Committee shall be 15. (3) The Managing Director of the Company shall be the Chief Executive of the Exchange. (3A) Notwithstanding anything contained herein, the SEBI circulars or directives dealing with the constitution, composition of the Executive Committee(s) of the Futures & Options segment and/or Currency Derivatives segment shall be complied with. Powers of Executive Committee (4) The Board may delegate from time to time to the Executive Committee(s) such of the powers vested in it and upon such terms as it may think fit, to manage all or any of the affairs of the Exchange and from time to time, to revoke, withdraw, alter or vary all or any of such powers. (5) The Executive Committee of each trading segment shall have such responsibilities and powers as may be delegated to it by the Board from time to time which may, inter alia, include the following responsibilities and powers to be discharged in accordance with the provisions of the Bye Laws and Rules : (a) approving securities for admission to the relevant Official List for NSE securities; (b) admitting trading members; 4 (c) approving, in the case of capital market trading segment, market-makers to act as such; (d) supervising the market and promulgating such Business Rules and Codes of Conduct as it may deem fit; (e) determining from time to time, fees, deposits, margins and other monies payable to the NSE by trading members and Companies whose securities are admitted/to be admitted to the Official List and the scale of brokerage chargeable by trading members; (f) prescribing, from time to time, capital adequacy and other norms which shall be required to maintained by trading members; (g) prescribing, from time to time, and administering and effecting penalties, fines and other consequences, including suspension/ expulsion for defaults or violation of any requirements of the Bye-laws and Regulations and the Rules and Codes of Conduct and criteria for readmission, if any, promulgated thereunder; (h) administering, maintaining and investment of the corpus of the Fund(s) set up by the Exchange including Investor Protection Fund; (i) norms, procedures and other matters relating to arbitration; (j) power to take disciplinary action/proceed legally against any trading member; (k) dissemination of information, announcements to be placed on the trading system; (l) listing requirements and conditions to be complied with; (m) listing fees payable by the company whose securities are admitted to dealings on the Exchange; (n) continuance of listed status of the company whose securities are admitted to dealings on the Exchange; (o) any other matter delegated by the Board. (6) The Executive Committee may from time to time constitute such sub-committees to carry on business complying with all regulations and guidelines laid down by the Executive Committee. The constitution, quorum and responsibilities of such sub committees will be determined by Executive Committee. (7) The Executive Committee may from time to time, authorise the Managing Director or such other person(s) to carry out such acts, deeds and functions in accordance with such provisions as may be laid down in this regard for fulfilling the responsibilities and discharging the powers delegated to it by the Board. (8) The Executive Committee(s) shall be bound and obliged to carry out and implement any directives issued by the Board from time to time and shall be 5 Bound to comply with all conditions of delegation and limitations on the powers of the Executive Committee(s) as may be prescribed. Government/SEBI Representative (9) The Government and SEBI shall nominate on the Executive Committee from time to time, not more than one person each to be referred to as “Government Nominee”. (10) Any vacancy caused by resignation, withdrawal of nomination, death or otherwise of such a nominated Government Representative shall be filled in by a similarly nominated person. Trading Members (11) Subject to provisions of Rules 18 and 19 herein, the Board shall nominate on the Executive Committee from time to time not more than four trading members. The persons so nominated shall hold office for a period of one year and shall be eligible for renomination. (12) Any vacancy caused by resignation, removal, death or otherwise of such a nominated person shall be filled in by a similarly nominated person. Public Representatives (13) The Board shall nominate on the Executive Committee from time to time not more than four persons referred to as ‘Public Representatives’ who are individual persons of eminence in the field of finance, accounting, law or other discipline. The persons so nominated shall hold office for a period of one year and shall be eligible for renomination. (14) Any vacancy caused by resignation, removal, death or otherwise of such a nominated Public Representative shall be filled in by a similarly nominated person. Other Nominees (15) The Board shall nominate on the Executive Committee from time to time not more than four persons referred to as ‘Other nominees’. These may include two senior officers of the Company. The persons so nominated shall hold office for a period of one year and shall be eligible for renomination. (16) Any vacancy caused by resignation, removal, death or otherwise of such a nominated person shall be filled in by a similarly nominated person. 6 Vacation of Office of Nominees of the Board (17) The office of nominees of the Board including that of the public representatives, trading members and other nominees on the Executive Committee shall ipso facto be vacated if: (a) he is adjudicated insolvent; (b) he applied to be adjudicated insolvent; (c) he is convicted by any Court in India of any offence and sentenced in respect thereof to imprisonment for not less than 30 days; (d) he absents himself from three consecutive meetings of the Executive Committee or for a continuous period of three months whichever is longer without obtaining leave of absence from the Committee meeting; (e) in the case of a trading member, if he ceases to be a trading member of the Exchange or if he, by notice in writing addressed to the Executive Committee, resigns his office or if he is suspended or expelled or if his membership is terminated; Provided however that if at any time the Board is satisfied that circumstances exist which render it necessary in public interest to do so, the Board may revoke the nomination of any such person. Eligibility of Trading Member to become Executive Committee member (18) No trading member shall be eligible to be nominated as a member of an Executive Committee:- (a) unless he satisfies the requirement, if any, prescribed in that behalf by the Rules framed under the Securities Contracts (Regulation) Act, 1956 and the Securities and Exchange Board of India Act, 1992; (b) unless he is a trading member of the relevant trading segment for such period as may be decided by the Board from time to time; (c) if he is a partner with a trading member who is already a member of that Executive Committee; (d) if he has at any time been declared as defaulter or failed to meet his liabilities in ordinary course or compounded with his creditors; (18A) No trading member shall be eligible to continue or be nominated on the Executive Committee:- (a) if his certificate of registration as a stock broker has been cancelled by the Securities and Exchange Board of India or he has been expelled by the Exchange; (b) if his certificate of registration as a stock broker or his trading rights have been suspended by the Securities and Exchange Board of India or the 7 Exchange as the case may be or his membership rights have been suspended by the Exchange on account of any disciplinary action taken against him under the Rules, Regulations or Byelaws of the Exchange and two years have not elapsed from the date of expiry of such suspension of certificate of registration, trading rights or membership rights; (c) if he falls in the category of Notified Persons as per the Special Courts (Trial of Offences Relating to Transaction in Securities) Act, 1992 and two years have not elapsed from the date the member is denotified under the said Act. (19) A trading member nominated for two consecutive years as a member on an Executive Committee shall not be eligible to be nominated to the Executive Committee unless a period of two years has elapsed since his last nomination. Office Bearers of Executive Committee (20) The Executive Committee shall from time to time have the following officebearers namely, the Chairman and Vice Chairman. (21) The Managing Director of the Company shall be the Chairman of Executive Committee(s). (22) The Executive Committee shall elect one among themselves as the Vice Chairman. (23) The Vice Chairman so elected shall hold office for a period of one year and shall be eligible for re-election. (24) In the event of any casual vacancy arising in the office of the Vice-Chairman due to death, resignation or any other cause, the Executive Committee shall nominate a successor from among the members of the Executive Committee. (25) The persons nominated/elected as above in any casual vacancy shall hold office for the same period for which the office-bearer in whose place he was appointed would have held office if it had not been vacated as aforesaid. Meetings of the Executive Committee (26) The Executive Committee may meet at least once in every calendar month for the despatch of business, adjourn and otherwise regulate its meetings and proceedings as it thinks fit, and may determine the quorum necessary for the transaction of business. (27) The quorum for a meeting of the Executive Committee, shall be one-third of the total strength of the Executive Committee, any fraction being rounded off as one, or three members whichever is higher; provided that where at any time the number of interested members exceeds two-thirds of the total strength, then the number of remaining members, i.e., the number of members not interested shall be the quorum for the meeting. 8 (28) The Chairman or Vice-Chairman or any two members of the Executive Committee may at any time convene a meeting of the Executive Committee. (29) Questions arising at any meeting of the Executive Committee shall be decided by a majority of the votes cast excepting in cases where a larger majority is required by any provision of the Bye Laws, Rules and Regulations of the Exchange. In the case of equality of votes on matters which can be decided by a majority of votes, the Chairman presiding over the meeting shall have a second or casting vote. (30) At all meetings of the Executive Committee the Chairman shall ordinarily preside and in his absence the Vice-Chairman shall preside. If the Vice-Chairman also be not present at the meeting, the members of the Executive Committee present shall choose one from among themselves to be Chairman of such meeting. (31) Subject to the conditions stated elsewhere every member of the Executive Committee shall have only one vote whether on a show of hands or on a poll except that in the case of a poll resulting in equal votes, the Chairman who presides over the meeting shall have a casting vote. (32) No vote by proxy shall be allowed either on a show of hands or on a poll in respect of any matter. Chairman and Vice Chairman (33) The Chairman may assume and exercise all such powers and perform all such duties as may be delegated to him by the Executive Committee from time to time as provided in the Rules, Bye Laws and Regulations of the Exchange. (34) In the absence of the Chairman or on his inability to act, the Vice-Chairman, and in his absence or inability to act, his functions and powers shall be exercised by the senior available officer of the Company under the directions of the Executive Committee. (35) The Chairman, and in his absence the Vice-Chairman, shall be entitled to exercise any or all of the powers exercisable by the Executive Committee whenever he be of the opinion that immediate action is necessary, subject to such action being confirmed by the Executive Committee within twenty-four hours. (36) The Chairman and/or delegated authority shall represent the Exchange officially in all public matters. Provided that the Executive Committee may direct that on any matters or occasion the Chairman and/or other member or members of the Executive Committee shall represent the Exchange. (37) A meeting of the Executive Committee for the time being, at which a quorum is present shall be competent to exercise all or any of the authorities, powers and discretion for the time being vested in or exercisable by the Executive Committee generally. 9 III. TRADING MEMBERSHIP (1) The rights and privileges of a trading member shall be subject to the Bye Laws, Rules and Regulations of the Exchange. (2) All trading members of the Exchange shall have to register themselves prior to commencing operations on the Exchange, with the Securities and Exchange Board of India. Eligibility (3) The following persons shall be eligible to become trading members of the Exchange: (a) individuals (b) registered firms (c) Limited Liability Partnership (d) bodies corporate (e) companies as defined in the Companies Act, 1956 and (f) such other persons or entities as may be permitted under the Securities Contracts (Regulation) Rules, 1957 as amended from time to time. (4) In relation to Tri-Party Repo Market ("TRM"), all such persons shall be eligible to become Trading Members of the TRM segment of the Exchange as may be prescribed by the Exchange/the relevant authority by way of Circulars, Bye Laws, Rules and Regulations from time to time (5) No person shall be admitted as a trading member of the Exchange if such proposed member: (a) is an individual who has not completed 21 years of age; (b) is an individual who is engaged as a principal or employer in any business other than that of securities except as a broker or agent not involving any personal financial liability unless he undertakes on admission to severe his connection with such business; (c) is a body corporate who has committed any act which renders the person liable to be wound up under the provisions of the law; (d) is a body corporate who has had a provisional liquidator or receiver or official liquidator appointed to the person; (e) has been adjudged bankrupt or a receiving order in bankruptcy has been made against the person or the person has been proved to be insolvent even though he has obtained his final discharge; (f) has been convicted of an offence involving a fraud or dishonesty; 10 (g) has compounded with his creditors for less than full discharge of debts; (h) has been at any time expelled or declared a defaulter by any other Stock Exchange; (i) has been previously refused admission to membership unless the period of one year has elapsed since the date of rejection; (j) incurs such disqualification under the provisions of the Securities Contracts (Regulation) Act, 1956 or Rules made thereunder as disentitles such person from seeking membership of a stock exchange. (6) No individual person shall be eligible for admission to trading membership of the Exchange unless: (a) he has worked for not less than two years as a Partner with, or as an authorised assistant or authorised clerk or apprentice to a member of any recognised stock exchange and is duly registered with that Exchange, or (b) he agrees to work for a minimum period of two years as a partner or representative member with another member of the Exchange and to enter into transactions on the Exchange not in his own name but in the name of that member under whom he is working; or (c) he succeeds to the established business of a deceased or retiring member of the Exchange who is his father, uncle, brother or any other person who is in the opinion of the relevant authority, a close relative; Provided that the relevant authority may waive compliance with any or all of the foregoing conditions contained in this Rule and at their discretion waive the requirements set out above, if they are of the opinion that the person seeking is considered by the relevant authority to be otherwise qualified to be admitted as a member by reason of his means, position, integrity, knowledge and experience of business in securities. (6A)

No Limited Liability Partnership shall be eligible to be admitted to the trading membership of the Exchange unless (a) the Limited Liability Partnership is formed and registered under the Limited Liability Partnership Act, 2008 (b) the Limited Liability Partnership complies with the conditions laid down in Rule 8(6) of the Securities Contracts (Regulation) Rules, 1957 pertaining to Limited Liability Partnerships. (7) No person shall be eligible to be admitted to the trading membership of the Exchange unless the person satisfies : (a) the requirements prescribed in that behalf under the Securities Contracts (Regulation) Act, 1956, and the Rules framed thereunder and under the 11 Securities and Exchange Board of India Act, 1992, and (b) such additional eligibility criteria as the Board or relevant authority may prescribe for the different classes of trading members and trading segments from time to time. (7A) Certification No person shall be eligible to be admitted to the trading membership of the Exchange unless he has passed the Certification Programme conducted by the Exchange for such Trading segment of the Exchange as it may determine from time to time. (8) Unless otherwise specified by the relevant authority, membership for any person shall be restricted to only one trading segment. (9) Trading member of any trading segment may trade in NSE securities applicable to that segment. Admission (10) Any person desirous of becoming a trading member shall apply to the Exchange for admission to the trading membership of the relevant trading segment of the Exchange. Every applicant shall be dealt with by the relevant authority who shall be entitled to admit or reject such applications at its discretion. (11) The application shall be made in such formats as may be specified by the relevant authority from time to time for application for admission of trading members to each trading segment. (12) The application shall have to be submitted along with such fees, security deposit and other monies in such form and in such manner as may be specified by the relevant authority from time to time. (13) The applicant shall have to furnish such declarations as may be specified from time to time by the relevant authority. (14) The relevant authority shall have the right to call upon the applicant to pay such fees or deposit such additional security in cash or kind, to furnish any additional guarantee or to require the deposit of any building fund, computerisation fund, training fund or fee as the relevant authority may prescribe from time to time. (15) The relevant authority may admit the applicant to the trading membership of the Exchange provided that the person satisfies the eligibility conditions and other procedures and requirements of admission. The relevant authority may at its absolute discretion reject any application for admission without communicating the reason thereof. (16) If for any reason the application is rejected, the admission fee shall be refunded to 12 the applicant, without any interest. (17) The relevant authority may at any time from the date of admission to the trading membership of the Exchange cancel the admission and expel a trading member if he has in or at the time of his application for admission to membership or during the course of the inquiry made by the relevant authority preceding his admission : (a) made any willful misrepresentation; or (b) suppressed any material information required of him as to his character and antecedents; or (c) has directly or indirectly given false particulars or information or made a false declaration. (18) When a person is admitted to the trading membership of the Exchange, intimation of the person's admission shall be sent to the person and to the Securities and Exchange Board of India. If the person admitted to the membership of the Exchange and after intimation of his admission is duly sent, does not become a member by complying with acts and procedures for exercising the privileges of membership as may be prescribed by the relevant authority within a specified time period from the date of despatch of the intimation of admission, the admission fee paid by him shall be forfeited by the Exchange. (19) (a) Every trading member of the Exchange shall, upon being admitted as a trading member of the Exchange be issued a certificate or entitlement slip as proof of having been admitted to the benefits and privileges of the trading membership of the Exchange. Such a certificate or entitlement slip shall not be transferable or transmittable except as herein mentioned. (b) Subject to such terms and conditions as the relevant authority may prescribe from time to time and to the prior written approval of the relevant authority, transfer of the certificate / entitlement slip, may be effected as follows: (i) by making nomination under these Rules; (ii) by an amalgamation or merger of a trading member company; (iii) by takeover of a trading member company; (iv) by transfer of the trading membership of a trading member firm to a new firm, in which, all the existing partners are not partners; and (v) by two or more trading members / trading member firms coming together to form a new partnership firm/company. (c) A Trading Member or his successor(s) may make a nomination to the certificate / entitlement slip of trading membership. The nomination(s) made by a trading member or successor(s) of a trading member shall be subject to the following conditions, namely: (i) The nominee(s) shall, at the time when the nomination becomes effective, be person(s) who shall be qualified to be admitted as 13 trading member(s) of the Exchange; (ii) The nominee(s) shall give to the relevant authority his/their unconditional and irrevocable acceptance of his/their nomination; (iii) A trading member shall nominate one or more of his successor(s) as per the applicable succession laws. If the trading member has no successor(s) willing to carry on the trading membership, then, the trading member may nominate person(s) other than his successor(s); (iv) If the trading member has not nominated any person and is rendered incompetent to carry on his business on the Exchange on account of physical disability, then the trading member may, within a period of six months, make a nomination as per the provisions of sub-clause (iii) above; (v) If the trading member has not nominated any person, the successor(s) of the trading member may nominate one or more persons from among themselves within six months from the date of the death of the trading member; (vi) If the nomination of the trading member is such that it cannot be given effect to by the relevant authority, at the time when the nomination would have become effective, then the successor(s) of such a trading member may nominate any other person(s) within six months from the date on which the nomination would have become effective; (vii) If more than one person(s) are nominated by the trading member or the successor(s), then such nominated person(s) shall be required to form a company to carryon the trading membership; (viii) A nomination made by a trading member or successor(s) may be revoked with the prior written approval of the relevant authority and subject to such terms and conditions as the relevant authority may prescribe from time to time. No such revocation shall be permitted after the nomination becomes effective; and (ix)

The nomination shall become effective in the case of a nomination made by a trading member, from the date of his death or physical disability or from the date of approval by the relevant authority, whichever is later and in the case of a nomination made by successor(s), from the date on which such nomination is made or from the date of approval by the relevant authority, whichever is later. (d) The relevant authority may permit the transfer of the certificate / entitlement slip in the following circumstances: (i) Death of a trading member; (ii) If in the opinion of the relevant authority, the trading member is rendered incompetent to carry on his business on the Exchange on 14 account of physical disability; (iii) Upon amalgamation or merger of a trading member company; (iv) Upon takeover of a trading member company; and (v) Upon the death of or resignation or notice of dissolution by a partner of a trading member firm, and re-alignment, if any, by the partners in such firm or by the partners in such firm and the nominee(s)/successor(s) of the outgoing partner or by the partners in such firm and person(s) other than the nominee(s)/successor(s) of the outgoing partner in a new firm, within a period of six months from the date of such death or resignation or notice of dissolution. (e) The relevant authority may, while permitting the transfer, prescribe from time to time such transfer fee as it deems fit in the following circumstances viz., (i) nomination by a trading member of a person other than successor(s) under the applicable laws; (ii) nomination by the successor(s) of a trading member, if the nominee(s) is/are not from amongst the successors; (iii) amalgamation or merger of a trading member company with a non trading member company resulting in the loss of majority shareholding and/ or control of management by the majority shareholders of the trading member company; (iv) takeover of the trading member company by non trading member(s) resulting in the loss of majority shareholding and/ or control of management by the majority shareholders of the trading member company; and (v) in the case of sub-clause (v) of clause (d), if the person(s) other than the nominee(s)/successor(s) of the outgoing partner hold atleast 51% of share in the profits & losses of the new firm and /or atleast 51% of share in the capital of the new firm. Explanation I For the purpose of sub-clauses (iii) and (iv) above, the term "loss of majority shareholding" means a shareholder or a group of shareholders holding 51% or more shares / interest in the trading member company ceases to hold 51% of shares / interest in the trading member company or in the amalgamated company which shall take up trading membership upon amalgamation of the trading member company with a non trading member company. Explanation II For the purpose of sub-clauses (iii) and (iv) above, the term "loss of control in management "means the loss of the right to appoint majority of the directors or to control the management or policy decision exercisable by person or persons acting individually or in concert, directly or indirectly including by virtue of their 15 shareholding or management rights or shareholders agreements or voting agreements or in any other manner. (f) For the purpose of the clauses (b) to (e), the term 'trading member' shall to the extent applicable, include a partner of a trading member firm or a shareholder of a trading member company. The term successor(s) shall to the extent applicable, include successor(s) of a partner of a trading member firm or successor(s) of a shareholder of a trading member company. (g) Without prejudice to any other provision of the Rules, the trading membership may be suspended, for such period as the relevant authority may deem fit, in the following circumstances: (i) Upon the individual trading member or a partner of a trading member firm or a shareholder of a trading member company, in the opinion of the relevant authority, being rendered incompetent to carryon his business on account of physical disability; (ii) Upon the mental disability of the individual trading member or a partner of a trading member firm provided the partner holds atleast 51% of share in the profits & losses of and/or atleast 51% of share in the capital of such firm or a shareholder of a trading member company provided the shareholder is a majority shareholder in such trading member company; (iii) Upon the death of an individual trading member or a partner of a trading member firm provided the partner holds atleast 51% of share in the profits & losses of and / or atleast 51% of share in the capital of such firm or a shareholder of a trading member company, provided the shareholder is a majority shareholder in such trading member company and during the six month period within which successor(s) of such individual trading member or partner or shareholder, may nominate person(s) to take up the stake/ shares of such deceased individual trading member or partner or shareholder; (iv) Upon the dissolution of a trading member firm and during the six month period as referred to in sub clause (v) of clause (d); and (v) Upon any deadlock in the management of a trading member firm or trading member company, which, in the opinion of the relevant authority will affect the ability of such trading member firm or trading member company to carry on its business. The trading member shall be entitled for an opportunity for representation before the relevant authority, before being suspended under this subclause, but the decision of the relevant authority shall be final. Explanation I For the purposes of this sub-clause, the term "Deadlock in the Management " means a situation wherein there is a loss of confidence or disagreement among the partners of a trading member firm or among the directors/shareholders of a trading 16 member company, which, in the opinion of the relevant authority, will affect or is likely to affect the conduct of business by the trading member firm or trading member company, as the case may be or an equality of vote at a meeting of the directors or shareholders of a trading member company. (h) Without prejudice to any other provision of the Rules, the trading membership may be terminated by the relevant authority if an acceptable nomination or realignment, as the case may be, does not take place to the satisfaction of the relevant authority, within the said period of six months. (i) The nominee(s), successor(s), partners of a trading member firm or such other persons, as the case may be shall be entitled for an opportunity for representation before the relevant authority, before being terminated under clause (h) above, but the decision of the relevant authority shall be final. Conversion of legal status of the trading member. (j) Subject to such terms and conditions as the relevant authority may prescribe from time to time and to the prior written approval of the relevant authority, conversion of the legal status of a trading member may be effected as follows: (i) by conversion of an individual trading member into a partnership firm / company; (ii) by conversion of a Trading Member firm into a company. (k) The relevant authority may permit the conversion of the legal status of the trading member in the following circumstances: (i) In the case of sub-clause (i) of clause (j), if the individual trading member holds and continues to hold atleast 51% of the share in the profits/losses and/or atleast 51% of share in the capital of the partnership firm, or atleast 51% of shareholding / interest in the company, which shall take up the trading membership of the Exchange. (ii) In the case of sub-clause (ii) of clause (j), if the partners holding atleast 51% of share in the profits / losses and /or atleast 51% of share in the capital of the trading member firm hold and continue to hold atleast 51% of shareholding / interest in the company which shall take up the trading membership of the Exchange. (20) The entitlement slip does not confer any ownership right as a member of the Company. The original of the entitlement slip shall stand deposited with the relevant authority. An authenticated photocopy or duplicate of such entitlement slip shall remain in the possession of the trading member as a proof of the trading membership of the Exchange. (21) A trading member shall not assign, mortgage, pledge, hypothecate or charge his 17 right of membership or any rights or privileges attached thereto and no such attempted assignment mortgage, pledge, hypothecation or charge shall be effective as against the Exchange for any purpose, nor shall any right or interest in any trading membership other than the personal right or interest of the trading member therein be recognised by the Exchange. The relevant authority shall expel any trading member of the Exchange who acts or attempts to act in violation of the provisions of this Rule. Partnership (22) No trading member shall form a partnership or admit a new partner to an existing partnership or make any change in the name of an existing partnership without intimation and prior approval of the relevant authority in such form and manner and subject to such requirements as the relevant authority may specify from time to time; these requirements may, inter alia, include deposits, declarations, guarantees and other conditions to be met by and which may be binding on partners of the firm who are not trading members. (23) No trading member shall, at the same time, be a partner in more than one partnership firm which is a trading member of the Exchange. (24) No trading member who is a partner in any partnership firm shall assign or in any way encumber his interest in such partnership firm. (25) The partnership firm shall register with the Income Tax authorities and with the Registrar of Firms and shall produce a proof of such registration to the Exchange. (26) The partners of the firm shall do business only on account of the firm and jointly in the name of the partnership firm. (27) The members of the partnership firm must communicate to the Exchange in writing under the signatures of all the partners or surviving partners any change in such partnership either by dissolution or retirement or death of any partner or partners. (28) Any notice of the Exchange intimating dissolution of a partnership shall contain a statement as to who undertakes the responsibility of settling all outstanding contracts and liabilities of the dissolved partnership firm but that shall not be deemed to absolve the other partner or partners of his or their responsibility for such outstanding contracts and liabilities. Termination of membership (29) Any trading member may cease to be a member, if one or more apply: (a) by resignation; (b) by death; 18 (c) by expulsion in accordance with the provisions contained in the Bye Laws, Rules and Regulations; (d) by being declared a defaulter in accordance with the Bye Laws, Rules and Regulations of the Exchange; (e) by dissolution in case of partnership firm; (f) by winding up or dissolution of such company in case of a limited company. Resignation (30) (a) A trading member who intends to resign from the trading membership of the Exchange shall intimate to the Exchange a written notice to that effect which shall be displayed on the trading system. (b) Any member of the Exchange objecting to any such resignation shall communicate the grounds of his objection to the relevant authority by letter within such period as may be specified by the relevant authority from time to time. (c) The relevant authority may accept the resignation of a member either unconditionally or on such conditions as it may think fit or may refuse to accept such resignation and in particular may refuse to accept such resignation until it is satisfied that all outstanding transactions with such member have been settled. Death (31) On the death of a member, his legal representatives and authorised representatives, if any, shall communicate due intimation thereof to the relevant authority in writing. Failure to pay Charges (32) Save as otherwise provided in the Bye Laws, Rules and Regulations of the Exchange if a member fails to pay his annual subscription, fees, charges or other monies which may be due by him to the Exchange or to the Clearing House within such time as the relevant authority may prescribe from time to time after notice in writing has been served upon him by the Exchange, he may be suspended by the relevant authority until he makes payment and if within a further period of fifteen days he fails to make such payment, he may be expelled by the relevant authority. Continued Admittance (33) The relevant authority shall from time to time prescribe conditions and requirements for continued admittance to trading membership which may, inter alia, include maintenance of minimum networth and capital adequacy, renewal of 19 certification, if any, etc. The trading membership of any person who fails to meet these requirements shall be liable to be terminated. Readmission of Defaulters (34) A trading member's right of membership shall lapse and vest with the Exchange immediately he is declared a defaulter. The member who is declared a defaulter shall forfeit all his rights and privileges as a member of the Exchange, including any right to use of or any claim upon or any interest in any property or funds of the Exchange, if any. (35) The relevant authority may readmit a defaulter as a trading member subject to the provisions as may be prescribed by the relevant authority from time to time. (36) The relevant authority may readmit only such defaulter who in its opinion: (a) has paid up all dues to the Exchange, other trading members and constituents; (b) has no insolvency proceedings against him in a Court or has not been declared insolvent by any Court; (c) has defaulted owing to the default of principals whom he might have reasonably expected to be good for their commitments; (d) has not been guilty of bad faith or breach of the Bye Laws, Rules and Regulations of the Exchange; (e) has been irreproachable in his general conduct. 20 IV. DISCIPLINARY PROCEEDINGS, PENALTIES, SUSPENSION AND EXPULSION Disciplinary Jurisdiction (1) The relevant authority may expel or suspend and/or fine under censure and/or warn and/or withdraw any of the membership rights of a trading member if it be guilty of contravention, non-compliance, disobedience, disregard or evasion of any of the Bye Laws, Rules and Regulations of the Exchange or of any resolutions, orders, notices, directions or decisions or rulings of the Exchange or the relevant authority or of any other Committee or officer of the Exchange authorised in that behalf or of any conduct, proceeding or method of business which the relevant authority in its absolute discretion deems dishonorable, disgraceful or unbecoming a trading member of the Exchange or inconsistent with just and equitable principles of trade or detrimental to the interests, good name or welfare of the Exchange or prejudicial or subversive to its objects and purposes. Penalty for Misconduct, Unbusinesslike Conduct and Unprofessional Conduct (2) In particular and without in any way limiting or prejudicing the generality of the provisions in Rule (1) above, a trading member shall be liable to expulsion or suspension or withdrawal of all or any of its membership rights and/or to payment of a fine and/or to be censured, reprimanded or warned for any misconduct, unbusinesslike conduct or unprofessional conduct in the sense of the provision in that behalf contained herein. Misconduct (3) A trading member shall be deemed guilty of misconduct for any of the following or similar acts or omissions namely: (a) Fraud : If it is convicted of a criminal offence or commits fraud or a fraudulent act which in the opinion of the relevant authority renders it unfit to be a trading member; (b) Violation : If it has violated provisions of any statute governing the activities, business and operations of the Exchange, trading members and securities business in general; (c) Improper Conduct : If in the opinion of the relevant authority it is guilty of dishonourable or disgraceful or disorderly or improper conduct on the Exchange or of willfully obstructing the business of the Exchange; (d) Breach of Rules, Bye Laws and Regulations : If it shields or assists or omits to report any trading member whom it has known to have committed a breach or evasion of any Rule, Bye-law and Regulation of the Exchange or of any resolution, order, notice or direction thereunder of the relevant authority or of any Committee or officer or the Exchange authorised in that behalf; 21 (e) Failure to comply with Resolutions : If it contravenes or refuses or fails to comply with or abide by any resolution, order, notice, direction, decision or ruling of the relevant authority or of any Committee or officer of the Exchange or other person authorised in that behalf under the Bye Laws, Rules and Regulations of the Exchange; (f) Failure to submit to or abide by Arbitration : If it neglects or fails or refuses to submit to arbitration or to abide by or carry out any award, decision or order of the relevant authority or the Arbitration Committee or the arbitrators made in connection with a reference under the Bye Laws, Rules and Regulations of the Exchange; (g) Failure to testify or give information : If it neglects or fails or refuses to submit to the relevant authority or to a Committee or an officer of the Exchange authorised in that behalf, such books, correspondence, documents and papers or any part thereof as may be required to be produced or to appeal and testify before or cause any of its partners, attorneys, agents, authorised representatives or employees to appear and testify before the relevant authority or such Committee or officer of the Exchange or other person authorised in that behalf; (h) Failure to submit Special Returns : If it neglects or fails or refuses to submit to the relevant authority within the time notified in that behalf special returns in such form as the relevant authority may from time to time prescribe together with such other information as the relevant authority may require whenever circumstances arise which in the opinion of the relevant authority make it desirable that such special returns or information should be furnished by any or all the trading members; (i) Failure to submit Audited Accounts: If it neglects or fails or refuses to submit its audited accounts to the Exchange within such time as may be prescribed by the relevant authority from time to time. (j) Failure to compare or submit accounts with Defaulter: If it neglects or fails to compare its accounts with the Member and Core Settlement Guarantee Fund Committee or to submit to it a statement of its accounts with a defaulter or a certificate that it has no such account or if it makes a false or misleading statement therein; (k) False or misleading Returns: If it neglects or fails or refuses to submit or makes any false or misleading statement in its clearing forms or returns required to be submitted to the Exchange under the Bye Laws, Rules and Regulations; (l) Vexatious complaints : If it or its agent brings before the relevant authority or a Committee or an officer of the Exchange or other person authorised in that behalf a charge, complaint or suit which in the opinion of the relevant authority is frivolous, vexatious or malicious; (m) Failure to pay dues and fees : If it fails to pay its subscription, fees, arbitration charges or any other money which may be due by it or any fine 22 or penalty imposed on it. Unbusinesslike Conduct (4) A trading member shall be deemed guilty of unbusinesslike conduct for any of the following or similar acts or omissions namely: (a) Fictitious Names : If it transacts its own business or the business of its constituent in fictitious names or if he carries on business in more than one trading segment of the Exchange under fictitious names; (b) Fictitious Dealings : If it makes a fictitious transaction or gives an order for the purchase or sale of securities the execution of which would involve no change of ownership or executes such an order with knowledge of its character; (c) Circulation of rumours : If it, in any manner, circulates or causes to be circulated, any rumours; (d) Prejudicial Business : If it makes or assists in making or with such knowledge is a party to or assists in carrying out any plan or scheme for the making of any purchases or sales or offers of purchase or sale of securities for the purpose of upsetting the equilibrium of the market or bringing about a condition in which prices will not fairly reflect market values; (e) Market Manipulation and Rigging : If it, directly or indirectly, alone or with other persons, effects series of transactions in any security to create actual or apparent active trading in such security or raising or depressing the prices of such security for the purpose of inducing purchase or sale of such security by others; (f) Unwarrantable Business : If it engages in reckless or unwarrantable or unbusinesslike dealings in the market or effects purchases or sales for its constituent's account or for any account in which it is directly or indirectly interested which purchases or sales are excessive in view of its constituent's or his own means and financial resources or in view of the market for such security; (g) Compromise : If it connives at a private failure of a trading member or accepts less than a full and bona fide money payment in settlement of a debt due by a trading member arising out of a transaction in securities; (h) Dishonoured Cheque : If it issues to any other trading member or to its constituents a cheque which is dishonored on presentation for whatever reasons; (i) Failure to carry out transactions with Constituents : If it fails in the opinion of the relevant authority to carry out its committed transactions with its constituents; 23 Unprofessional Conduct (5) A trading member shall be deemed guilty of unprofessional conduct for any of the following or similar acts or omissions namely: (a) Business in Securities in which dealings not permitted : If it enters into dealings in securities in which dealings are not permitted; (b) Business for Defaulting Constituent : If it deals or transacts business directly or indirectly or executes an order for a constituent who has within its knowledge failed to carry out engagements relating to securities and is in default to another trading member unless such constituent shall have made a satisfactory arrangement with the trading member who is its creditor; (c) Business for Insolvent : If without first obtaining the consent of the relevant authority it directly or indirectly is interested in or associated in business with or transacts any business with or for any individual who has been bankrupt or insolvent even though such individual shall have obtained his final discharge from an Insolvency Court; (d) Business without permission when under suspension : If without the permission of the relevant authority it does business on its own account or on account of a principal with or through a trading member during the period it is required by the relevant authority to suspend business on the Exchange; (e) Business for or with suspended, expelled and defaulter trading members : If without the special permission of the relevant authority it shares brokerage with or carries on business or makes any deal for or with any trading member who has been suspended, expelled or declared a defaulter; (f) Business for Employees of other trading members : If it transacts business directly or indirectly for or with or executes an order for an authorised representative or employee of another trading member without the written consent of such employing trading member; (g) Business for Exchange Employees : If it makes a speculative transaction in which an employee of the Exchange is directly or indirectly interested; (h) Advertisement : If it advertises for business purposes or issues regularly circular or other business communications to persons other than its own constituents, trading members of the Exchange, Banks and Joint Stock

Companies or publishes pamphlets, circular or any other literature or report or information relating to the stock markets without the prior written permission of the Exchange or in contravention of the advertisement code prescribed by the Exchange; (i) Evasion of Margin Requirements : If it willfully evades or attempts to evade or assists in evading the margin requirements prescribed in these Bye Laws and Regulations; 24 (j) Brokerage Charge: If it willfully deviates from or evades or attempts to evade the Bye Laws and Regulations relating to charging and sharing of brokerage. (k) Dealings with entities prohibited to buy or sell or deal in securities market: If it deals, directly or indirectly, in the course of its business with or transacts any business with or for any entity, which has been prohibited by SEBI to buy or sell or deal in the securities market. Trading member's responsibility for Partners, Agents and Employees (6) A trading member shall be fully responsible for the acts and omissions of its authorised officials, attorneys, agents, authorised representatives and employees and if any such act or omission be held by the relevant authority to be one which if committed or omitted by the trading member would subject it to any of the penalties as provided in the Bye Laws, Rules and Regulations of the Exchange then such trading member shall be liable therefor to the same penalty to the same extent as if such act or omission had been done or omitted by itself. Suspension on failure to provide margin deposit and/or Capital Adequacy requirements (7) The relevant authority shall require a trading member to suspend its business when it fails to provide the margin deposit and/ or meet capital adequacy norms as provided in these Bye Laws, Rules and Regulations and the suspension of business shall continue until it furnishes the necessary margin deposit or meet capital adequacy requirements. The relevant authority may expel a trading member acting in contravention of this provision. Suspension of Business: (8) The relevant authority may require a trading member to suspend its business in part or in whole : (a) Prejudicial Business : When in the opinion of the relevant authority, the trading member conducts business in a manner prejudicial to the Exchange by making purchases or sales of securities or offers to purchase or sell securities for the purpose of upsetting equilibrium of the market or bringing about a condition of demoralisation in which prices will not fairly reflect market values, or (b) Unwarrantable Business : When in the opinion of the relevant authority it engages in unwarrantable business or effects purchases or sales for its constituent's account or for any account in which it is directly or indirectly interested which purchases or sales are excessive in view of its constituent's or its own means and financial resources or in view of the market for such security, or (c) Unsatisfactory Financial Condition : When in the opinion of the relevant 25 authority it is in such financial condition that it cannot be permitted to do business with safety to its creditors or the Exchange. Removal of Suspension (9) The suspension of business under clause (8) above shall continue until the trading member has been allowed by the relevant authority to resume business on its paying such deposit or on its doing such act or providing such thing as the relevant authority may require. Penalty for Contravention (10) A trading member who is required to suspend its business shall be expelled by the relevant authority if he acts in contravention of this provision. Trading members and others to testify and give information (11) A trading member shall appear and testify before and cause its partners, attorneys, agents, authorised representatives and employees to appear and testify before the relevant authority or before other Committee(s) or an officer of the Exchange authorised in that behalf and shall produce before the relevant authority or before other Committee(s) or an officer of the Exchange authorised in that behalf, such books, correspondence, documents, papers and records or any part thereof which may be in its possession and which may be deemed relevant or material to any matter under inquiry or investigation. Permission necessary for Legal Representation (12) No person shall have the right to be represented by professional counsel, attorney, advocate or other representative in any investigation or hearing before the relevant authority or any other Committee unless the relevant authority or other Committee so permits. Explanation before suspension or expulsion (13) A trading member shall be entitled to be summoned before the relevant authority and afforded an opportunity for explanation before being suspended or expelled but in all cases the findings of the relevant authority shall be final and conclusive. Temporary Suspension (13 A) (a) Notwithstanding what is contained in clause (13) herein above if in the opinion of the Managing Director it is necessary to do so, he may, for reasons to be recorded in writing, temporarily suspend a trading member, pending completion of the proceedings for suspension under this chapter by the relevant authority, and no notice of hearing shall be required for such temporary suspension and such temporary suspension shall have the same consequences of suspension under this chapter. 26 (b) A notice to show cause shall be issued to the trading member within five working days of such temporary suspension. (c) Any such temporary suspension may be revoked at the discretion of the Managing Director, for reasons to be recorded in writing, if the Managing Director is satisfied that the circumstances leading to the formations of opinion of the Managing Director to effect temporary suspension, have ceased to exist or are satisfactorily resolved. (d) A trading member aggrieved by the temporary suspension may appeal to the relevant authority, provided that such appeal shall not automatically suspend the temporary suspension unless otherwise directed by the relevant authority. Effect of suspension of registration by SEBI (13B) Notwithstanding anything contained in any of the Byelaws and Rules of the Exchange, if the registration of a Trading Member is suspended by SEBI, such Trading Member shall ipso facto stand suspended from the trading membership of the Exchange for the period of suspension, so imposed by SEBI or till such suspension is in force. Imposition of Penalties (14) The penalty of suspension, withdrawal of all or any of the membership rights, fine, censure or warning may be inflicted singly or conjointly by the relevant authority. The penalty of expulsion may be inflicted by the relevant authority. Pre-determination of Penalties (15) The relevant authority shall have the power to pre-determine the penalties, the period of any suspension, the withdrawal of particular membership rights and the amount of any fine that would be imposed on contravention, non-compliance, disobedience, disregard or evasion of any Bye Law, Rules or Regulation of the Exchange or of any resolution, order, notice, direction, decision or ruling thereunder of the Exchange, the relevant authority or of any other Committee or officer of the Exchange authorised in that behalf. Commutation (16) Subject to the provision of the Securities Contracts (Regulation) Rules, 1957 the relevant authority in its discretion may in any case suspend a trading member in lieu of the penalty of expulsion or may withdraw all or any of the membership rights or impose a fine in lieu of the penalty of suspension or expulsion and may direct that the guilty trading member be censured or warned or may reduce or remit any such penalty on such terms and conditions as it deems fair and equitable. 27 Reconsideration/Review (17) Subject to the provisions of the Securities Contracts (Regulation) Rules, 1957 the relevant authority may of its own motion within 90 days from the date of communication of decision of the relevant authority to the member reconsider and may rescind, revoke or modify its resolution withdrawing all or any of the membership rights or fining, censuring or warning any trading member. In a like manner the relevant authority may rescind, revoke or modify its resolution expelling or suspending any trading member. Failure to pay fines and penalties (18) If a trading member fails to pay any fine or penalty imposed on it within such period as prescribed from time to time by the relevant authority after notice in writing has been served on it by the Exchange it may be suspended by the relevant authority until it makes payment and if within a further period as prescribed from time to time it fails to make such payment it may be expelled by the relevant authority. Consequence of Suspension (19) The suspension of a trading member shall have the following consequences namely: (a) Suspension of Membership Rights : The suspended trading member shall during the terms of its suspension be deprived of and excluded from all the rights and privileges of membership including the right to attend or vote at any meeting of the general body of trading members of the relevant segment, but it may be proceeded against by the relevant authority for any offence committed by it either before or after its suspension and the relevant authority shall not be debarred from taking cognizance of and adjudicating on or dealing with any claim made against it by other trading members; (b) Rights of creditors unimpaired : The suspension shall not affect the rights of the trading members who are creditors of the suspended trading member; (c) Fulfillment of Contracts : The suspended trading member shall be bound to fulfil contracts outstanding at the time of its suspension; (d) Further business prohibited : The suspended trading member shall not during the terms of its suspension make any trade or transact any business with or through a trading member provided that it may with the permission of the relevant authority close with or through a trading member the transactions outstanding at the time of its suspension; (e) Trading members not to deal : No trading member shall transact business for or with or share brokerage with a suspended trading member during 28 the terms of its suspension except with the previous permission of the relevant authority. Consequences of Expulsion (20) The expulsion of a trading member shall have the following consequences namely: (a) Trading membership Rights forfeited : The expelled trading member shall forfeit to the Exchange its right of trading membership and all rights and privileges as a trading member of the Exchange including an y right to the use of or an y claim upon or an y interest in an y property or funds of the Exchange but any liability of an y such trading member to the Exchange or to any trading member of the Exchange shall continue and remain unaffected by its expulsion; (b) Office vacated : The expulsion shall create a vacancy in any office or position held by the expelled trading member; (c) Rights of Creditors unimpaired : The expulsion shall not affect the rights of the trading members who are creditors of the expelled trading member; (d) Fulfillment of Contracts : The expelled trading member shall be bound to fulfil transactions outstanding at the time of his expulsion and it may with the permission of the relevant authority close such outstanding transactions with or through a trading member; (e) Trading members not to deal: No trading member shall transact business for or with or share brokerage with the expelled trading member except with the previous permission of the relevant authority. (f) Consequences of declaration of defaulter to follow: The provisions of Chapter XII and Chapter XIII of the Byelaws pertaining to default and Protection Fund respectively, shall become applicable to the Trading Member expelled from the Exchange as if such Trading Member has been declared a defaulter. Expulsion Rules to Apply (21) When a trading member ceases to be such under the provisions of these Bye Laws otherwise than by death, default or resignation it shall be as if such trading member has been expelled by the relevant authority and in that event all the provisions relating to expulsion contained in these Rules shall apply to such trading member in all respects. Suspension of Business (22) (a) The relevant authority shall require a trading member to suspend its business when it fails to maintain or provide further security as prescribed in the Bye Laws and Regulations and the suspension shall continue until it pays the necessary amount by way of security. 29 (b) Penalty for Contravention : A trading member who is required to suspend its business under clause (a) shall be expelled by the relevant authority if it acts in contravention of the provisions of the Bye Laws. Notice of Penalty and suspension of Business (23) Notice shall be given to the trading member concerned and to the trading members in general by a notice on the trading system of the Exchange of the expulsion or suspension or default of or of the suspension of business by a trading member or of any other penalty imposed on it or on its partners, attorneys, agents, authorised representatives or other employees. The relevant authority may in its absolute discretion and in such manner as it thinks fit notify or cause to be notified to the trading members of the Exchange or to the public that any person who is named in such notification has been expelled, suspended, penalised or declared a defaulter or has suspended its business or ceased to be a trading member. No action or other proceedings shall in any circumstances be maintainable by such person against the Exchange or the relevant authority or any officer or employee of the Exchange for the publication or circulation of such notification and the application for trading membership or the application for registration as the constituted attorney or authorised representative or by the person concerned shall operate as license and the Bye Laws, Rules and Regulations shall operate as leave to print, publish or circulate such advertisement or notification and be pleadable accordingly. (24) The Relevant authority for the purpose of this Chapter shall be the Member and Core Settlement Guarantee Fund Committee as may be constituted by the Board of Directors from time to time. The Composition of Member and Core Settlement Guarantee Fund Committee shall be such as may be prescribed by SEBI --- 30

CHAPTER SIX

NSE BYELAWS

NATIONAL STOCK EXCHANGE OF INDIA LIMITED BYE LAWS ARRANGEMENT OF CHAPTERS

DEFINITIONS (1) "Board" means Board of Directors of NSEIL. (2) "Exchange Securities" means securities which have been admitted to the Official List(s) of NSE Securities. (3) "Exchange" means the Stock Exchange(s) operated by NSEIL. (4) "Executive Committee" or "EC" means the Committee of the NSE formed in accordance with Chapter II. (5) "Issuer" includes a Government, a body corporate or other entity, whether incorporated or not, which issues any security or other instrument, or draws or accepts a negotiable instrument which is admitted to dealings on the NSE. (6) "Market-Maker" means a trading member registered under Chapter VIII. (7) "NSEIL" means the National Stock Exchange of India Limited. (8) "Official List of NSE securities" means the list of securities which are listed or permitted to trade on the Exchange. (9) "Participant" means a constituent who is registered by the relevant authority from time to time under Chapter VI of the ByeLaws. (10) "Regulations", unless the context indicates otherwise, includes business rules, code of conduct and such other regulations prescribed by the relevant authority from time to time for the operations of the Exchange and these shall be subject to the provisions of the Securities Contracts (Regulation) Act, 1956 and Rules and SEBI Act. (11) "Relevant Authority" means the Board, Securities and Exchange Board of India or such other authority as specified by the Board from time to time as relevant for a specified purpose. (12) "Relevant NSE Securities" or "Relevant Securities" means those NSE securities pertaining to the relevant trading segment. (13) "Rules", unless the context indicates otherwise, means rules as mentioned hereunder for regulating the activities and responsibilities of trading members of NSE and as prescribed by the relevant authority from time to time for the constitution, organisation and functioning of the Exchange and these rules shall be subject to the provisions of the Securities Contracts (Regulation) Act, 1956 and Rules and SEBI Act. (14) "SEBI" means the Securities and Exchange Board of India. (15) "Security(ies)" shall have the meaning assigned to it in the Securities Contracts (Regulation) Act, 1956 (as amended from time to time) and shall also include such other class of monetary transactions or instruments, scrip less or otherwise, as may be admitted to dealings on Exchange. (16) "Security admitted to dealings" includes a security which is listed or permitted to trade on Exchange. 3 Confidential (17) "Trading Member" means a Stock broker and the member of the NSE registered in accordance with Chapter V of the Bye-Laws and will include such an entity which is permitted by NSE to enter into Tri-party Repo transactions on the TRM segment. (18) "Trading Segments" or "Segments" mean the different segments or divisions comprising of NSE securities as may be classified and specified by the Board or relevant authority from time to time. (19) "Trading system of the NSE" means a system which makes available to trading members and the investing public, by whatever method, quotations in NSE securities and disseminates information regarding trades effected, volumes, etc. and such other notifications as may be placed thereon by the EC. (20) "Authorised Person" means any person - individual, partnership firm, LLP or body corporate – who is appointed as such by a stock broker (including trading member) and who provides access to trading platform of a stock exchange as an agent of the stock broker. 4 Confidential CHAPTER I TRADING SEGMENTS (1) There may be more than one trading segment as may be specified by the relevant authority from time to time. The Exchange shall seek the approval of SEBI before introducing any new trading segment. (2) The securities which will be eligible for admission to the different trading segments will be specified by the relevant authority from time to time. Wholesale Debt Market Segment (3) Instruments used for Wholesale Debt Market transactions may be admitted to dealings on the Wholesale Debt Market Trading Segment subject to trading regulations which the relevant authority may prescribe from time to time. Capital Market Trading Segment (4) Securities eligible under the Securities Contracts (Regulation) Act, 1956, may be admitted to dealings on the Capital Market Trading Segment. Futures & Options Trading segment (5) Derivatives contracts approved by SEBI may be admitted to dealings on the Futures & Options Trading Segment. Currency derivatives segment (6) Derivatives contracts based on currency or any other underlying approved by SEBI maybe admitted to dealings on the currency derivatives segment. SME Trading segment (7) The specified securities issued by the Small & Medium Enterprises in accordance with the Securities and Exchange Board of India (Issue of Capital and Disclosure

Requirements) Regulations, 2009 may be admitted to the dealings on the SME Trading segment. Commodity Derivative Segment (8) Derivative contracts based on commodity or any other underlying as approved by SEBI from time to time, may be admitted to dealing on the commodity derivatives segment Debt segment (9) Debt Securities and debt instruments may be admitted to dealings on the Debt Segment subject to such trading regulations which the relevant authority may prescribe from time to time. For the purpose of this Byelaw, Debt Securities and debt instruments shall include the following: (i) "debt securities" as defined in Securities and Exchange Board of India (Issue and Listing of Debt Securities) Regulations, 2008; 5 Confidential (ii) Government Securities, Treasury Bills, State Government loans, SLR and Non-SLR Bonds issued by Financial Institutions, municipal bonds, single bond repos, basket repos and CBLO kind of products subject to RBI approval, where required; (iii) Securitised debt instruments as defined in SEBI (Public Offer and Listing of Securitised Debt Instruments) Regulations,2008; (iv) Any other debt instruments as may be specified from time to time by the competent authority. (v) Such other debt securities as may be specified by the Relevant Authority from time to time with prior approval of SEBI. Tri-party Repo Market (“TRM”) Tri-party Repos on securities may be admitted to dealings on the TRM segment (under the Debt Segment). For the purpose of this Byelaw, securities admitted for trading on the TRM segment shall mean and include all such securities as may be notified by the relevant authority from time to time. (10) Further trading segments such as for debt instruments or equity instruments or any other segment maybe specified by the relevant authority from time to time. (11)

The Exchange, subject to prior approval of SEBI, may enter into such arrangement pursuant to proviso to Section 13 of the Securities Contracts (Regulation) Act, 1956 with one or more recognised stock exchanges. In such an event, the provisions of these Byelaws and Regulations shall apply subject to such modifications as maybe specified by Relevant Authority from time to time. 6 Confidential CHAPTER II EXECUTIVE COMMITTEE (1) Executive Committee(s) shall be appointed by the Board for the purposes of managing the day to day affairs of the different trading segment(s) in such manner as laid down in the Rules. (2) The Executive Committee of each trading segment shall have such responsibilities and powers as maybe delegated to it by the Board as provided for in the Rules. 7 Confidential CHAPTER III REGULATIONS (1) The Board or relevant authority may prescribe Regulations from time to time for the functioning and operations of the Exchange and to regulate the functioning and operations of the trading members of the Exchange. (2) Without prejudice to the generality of (1) above, the Board or relevant authority may prescribe regulations from time to time, inter alia, with respect to: (a) norms, procedures, terms and conditions to be complied with for inclusion of securities in the Official List of NSE securities; (b) fees payable by an Issuer for inclusion and continued inclusion in the Official List of NSE Securities; (c) norms and procedures for admission of trading members in accordance with ChapterV; (d) norms and procedures for approval of market-makers to act as such; (e) forms and conditions of contracts to be entered into, and the time, mode and manner for performance of contracts between trading members inter se or between trading members and their constituents; (f) determination from time to time, of fees, system usage charges, deposits, margins and other monies payable to the Exchange by trading members, participants and by Issuers whose securities are admitted/ to be admitted to dealings on the Exchange and the scale of brokerage chargeable by trading members; (g) prescription, from time to time, of capital adequacy and other norms which shall be required to be maintained by trading members; (h) supervision of the market and promulgation of such Business Rules and Codes of Conduct as it may deem fit; (i) maintenance of records and books of accounts by trading members as it may deem fit and records as required under the Securities Contracts (Regulation) Act and Rules and SEBI Act; (j) inspection and audit of records and books of accounts; (k) prescription, from time to time, and administration of penalties, fines and other consequences, including suspension/ expulsion for defaults or violation of any requirements of the Bye Laws and Regulations and the Rules and Codes of Conduct and criteria for readmission, if any, promulgated thereunder; (l) disciplinary action/ procedures against any trading member; 8 Confidential (m) settlement of disputes, complaints, claims arising between trading members inter- se as well as between trading members and persons who are not trading members relating to any transaction in securities made on the Exchange including settlement by arbitration; (n) norms and procedures for arbitration; (o) administration, maintenance and investment of the corpus of the Fund(s) set up by the Exchange including Investor Protection Fund; (p) norms and procedures for settlement and clearing of deals, including establishment and functioning of clearing house or other arrangements for clearing and settlement; (q) norms, procedures, terms and conditions for registration and continuance of registration of Participants; (r) norms and procedures in respect of, incidental or consequential to closing out of contracts, deals or transactions; (s) dissemination of information, announcements to be placed on the trading system; (t) any other matter as may be decided by the Board. 9 Confidential CHAPTER IV DEALINGS IN SECURITIES Dealings Allowed (1) Dealings in securities shall be permitted on the Exchange as provided in these Bye Laws and Regulations and save as so provided, no other dealings are permitted. Admission of Securities to Dealings (2) (a) Dealings are permitted on the Exchange in accordance with the provisions prescribed in these Bye Laws and Regulations in that behalf, in securities which are, from time to time, listed or permitted to trade on the trading segments by the relevant authority. (b) Admission of securities to listing on the Exchange shall be in accordance with provisions prescribed in these Bye Laws and Regulations in that behalf. (c) The relevant authority may admit from time to time securities which are permitted to trade on the Exchange. Government Securities (3) (a) Notwithstanding anything contained in Byelaw (2) above, dealings shall be deemed to have been permitted in Government securities, which term for the purpose of these Rules, Bye Laws and the Regulations made thereunder shall denote securities issued by the Government of India, State Governments, Port Trusts, Municipalities, local authorities, statutory bodies and similar other bodies or authorities and include treasury bills issued by the Government of India. (b) Government securities shall be deemed to have been admitted to dealing on such market segment of the Exchange as may be prescribed by the relevant authority as from the date of their inclusion on the Official List(s) of NSE Securities. Dealings in Securities Dealt on other Stock Exchanges (4) Without prejudice to the generality of Byelaw (2) above, the relevant authority may in its discretion and subject to such conditions as it may deem proper, permit dealings in any securities admitted to dealings on any other Stock Exchange or which are regularly dealt in on such Stock Exchange. Application for Admission to Listing (5) Applications for admission of securities to listing on the Exchange shall be made to the relevant authority in such form as the relevant authority may from time to time prescribe. Conditions and Requirements of Dealings (6) The relevant authority may not grant admission to dealings to the securities of an Issuer unless it complies with the conditions and requirements prescribed in these Bye Laws and Regulations and such other conditions and requirements as the relevant authority may from time to time prescribe. 10 Confidential Refusal of Admission to Listing (7) The relevant authority may, in its discretion, approve subject to such terms as it deems proper, or defer, or reject any application for admission of a security to listing on the Exchange. Fees (8) (a) Issuers whose securities are granted admission to dealings on the Exchange shall pay such listing and such other fees and such other deposits as the relevant authority may from time to time determine. (b) Every Issuer shall comply with the conditions of the Listing Agreement as prescribed by Exchange and/or SEBI from time to time and shall be liable to pay such fine(s) as may be prescribed by Exchange and/ or SEBI from time to time for non- compliance of provisions of the Listing Agreement or any of the SEBI Regulations dealing with listing as may be applicable to Issuers listed on Exchange. Dealings in Provisional

Documents (9) The relevant authority may, in its discretion, permit dealings in Provisional Documents. Provisional Documents for purposes of these Bye Laws and Regulations denote Coupons, Fractional Certificates, Letters of Renunciation or transferable Letters of Allotment, Acceptance or Application or options or other rights or interests in securities, warrants issued or to be issued by an issuer or other similar documents in respect of an issuer whose securities are sought to be admitted/ admitted to dealings on the Exchange. Issuers Registered Outside India (10) Admission to dealings on the Exchange shall not be granted to securities issued by a body corporate, fund or other entity registered or formed outside India unless: (a) there is adequate public interest in such securities in India; (b) the body corporate, fund or other entity agrees to maintain a register of members or other similar record in India and agrees to abide by such other criteria as prescribed by the relevant authority are satisfied. Specific Deals (11) The relevant authority may permit specific deals to be made in the case of securities of Issuers not admitted to dealings on the Exchange, which for the time being are prohibited or suspended fordealings. Prohibited Dealings (12) The relevant authority may prohibit dealings on the Exchange in any security or securities for any cause. Suspension of Admission to Dealings on the Exchange (13) (a) The relevant authority may suspend at any time the admission to dealings on the Exchange granted to any security for such period as it may determine. At the expiration 11 Confidential of the period of suspension the relevant authority may revoke the suspension subject to such conditions as it deems fit. (b) The manner of suspension and revocation of suspension of admission to dealings on the Exchange shall be in accordance with Standard Operating Procedure (SOP) prescribed by Exchange and/ or SEBI from time totime. Withdrawal of Admission to Dealings on Redemption or Conversion (14) The relevant authority may, if necessary, withdraw admission to dealings granted to securities which are about to be exchanged or converted into other securities as a result of any scheme of reorganisation or reconstruction or which being redeemable or convertible securities are about to fall due for redemption or conversion. Withdrawal of Admission to Dealings on Liquidation or Merger (15) If any issuer be placed in final or provisional liquidation or is about to be merged into or amalgamated with another entity, the relevant authority may withdraw the admission to dealings on the Exchange granted to its securities. The relevant authority may accept such evidence as it deems sufficient on such liquidation, merger or amalgamation. Should the merger or amalgamation fail to take place or should an issuer placed in provisional liquidation be reinstated and an application be made for readmission of its securities to dealings on the Exchange. The relevant authority shall have the right of approving, refusing or deferring such application. Withdrawal of Admission to Dealings on the Exchange (16) The relevant authority may, where deemed necessary, after giving an opportunity to the issuer to explain, withdraw the admission to dealings on the Exchange granted to its securities either for breach of or non-compliance with any of the conditions or requirements of admission to dealings, or for any other reason whatsoever. Readmission to Dealings on the Exchange (17) The relevant authority in its discretion may readmit to dealings on the Exchange the securities of an issuer whose admission to dealings has been previously withdrawn. 12 Confidential CHAPTER V

TRADING MEMBERS Appointment and Fees (1) (a) The relevant authority is empowered to admit trading members in accordance with the Bye Laws, Rules and Regulations it may frame from time to time in accordance with the Securities Contracts (Regulation) Act and Rules and the SEBI Act. (b) The relevant authority may specify prerequisites, conditions, formats and procedures for application for admission, termination, re-admission, etc. of trading members to each trading segment. The relevant authority may, at its absolute discretion, refuse permission to any applicant to be appointed as trading member. (c) The trading member shall pay such fees, security deposits and other monies as may be specified by the Board or the relevant authority from time to time, on admission as trading member and for continued admission. The fees, security deposits, other monies and any additional deposits paid, whether in the form of cash, Bank Guarantee, Securities or otherwise, with the Exchange, by a trading member from time to time, shall be subject to a first and paramount lien for any sum due to the Exchange and all other claims against the trading member for due fulfillment of engagements, obligations and liabilities of trading members arising out of or incidental to any dealings made subject to the Byelaws, Rules and Regulations of the Exchange. The Exchange shall be entitled to adjust or appropriate such fees, deposits and other monies for such dues and claims, to the exclusion of the other claims against the trading member, without any reference to the trading member. (d) Trading member of any trading segment may trade on the Exchange in the NSE securities applicable to that segment. (e) Trading members may trade in relevant securities either on their own account as principals or on behalf of their clients unless otherwise specified by the relevant authority and subject to such conditions which the relevant authority may prescribe from time to time. They may also act as market-makers in such securities if they are so authorised and subject to such conditions as under Chapter VIII. (f) Any bank included in the Second Schedule of the Reserve Bank of India Act, 1934, and specifically authorized by Reserve Bank of India for this purpose, i. is eligible to become a Trading Member of the currency derivatives segment of the Exchange, on the recommendation of the Relevant Authority. ii. such bank can act as a Trading Member for its proprietary dealings, to act on its own account, in the currency derivatives segment of the Exchange. iii. such bank can also act as a Trading Member for its clients or constituents in the currency derivatives segment of the Exchange. 13 Confidential iv such bank shall also abide by the circulars and directions issued by RBI and SEBI in respect of dealings of such bank on the Exchange besides Rules, Byelaws and Regulations of the Exchange. Conditions (2) (a) Trading members shall adhere to the Bye Laws, Rules and Regulations of the Exchange and shall comply with such operational parameters, rulings, notices, guidelines and instructions of the relevant authority as may be applicable. (b) All contracts issued for deals on the Exchange shall be in accordance with the Bye Laws, Rules and Regulations of the Exchange. (c) Trading members shall comply with such Exchange requirements as may be prescribed by the relevant authority from time to time with regard to advertisements and issue of circulars in connection with their activities as trading members. (d) Trading members shall furnish declarations relating to such matters and in such forms as may be prescribed by the relevant authority from time to time. (e) Trading members shall furnish to the Exchange an annual Auditors‘ Certificate certifying that specified Exchange requirements as may be prescribed from time to time by the relevant authority pertaining to their operations have been complied with. (f) Trading members shall furnish such information and periodic returns pertaining to their operations as may be required by the relevant authority from time to time. (g) Trading members shall furnish to the extent such audited and/or unaudited financial or quantitative information and statements as may be required by the relevant authority from time to time. (h) Trading members shall extend full co-operation and furnish such information and explanation as may be required for the purpose of any inspection or audit authorised by the relevant authority or other authorised official of the Exchange into or in regard to any trades, dealings, their settlement, accounting and/or other related matters. 14 Confidential CHAPTER VI PARTICIPANTS Registration of Participants on application (1) The relevant authority may register as a "Participant", those from amongst the constituents as are desirous of registering themselves as such, in accordance with these Bye Laws and Regulations framed from time to time, for such purpose and subject to such terms and conditions as may be prescribed by the relevant authority. Suo Moto Registration of Participant (2) Notwithstanding anything contained in Byelaw (1) above, the relevant authority may suo moto register as a 'Participant‘ those from amongst the constituents as, in the opinion of the relevant authority for reasons to be recorded, should be so registered, subject to such terms and conditions as may be prescribed by the relevant authority. Rights and Liabilities of Participants (3) (a) Notwithstanding any provisions to the contrary as may be contained in any other part of the B ye Laws especially

VII(3) (a), the Exchange may recognise a Participant as a party to the deal or trade made, firmed up or contracted by the Participant through a trading member on any segment of the Exchange, for such purposes (including for clearing and settlement) subject to such terms, conditions and requirements and in such circumstances as may be prescribed by the relevant authority from time to time. (b) Save as otherwise provided in these Bye Laws and Regulations, recognition of the Participant by the Exchange as a party to the deal or trade made, firmed up or contracted by the Participant through the trading member, shall not in any way affect the jurisdiction of the Exchange on the concerned trading member in regard thereto and such trading member shall continue to remain responsible, accountable and liable to the Exchange in this behalf. (4) The relevant authority may prescribe from time to time such guidelines governing the functioning and operation of the Participants on the Exchange and conditions for continuance of their registration or recognition. Without prejudice to the generality of the foregoing, such norms, requirements and conditions may include prescription of, inter alia, deposits, margins, fees, system usage charges, system maintenance/propriety, etc. (5) Rights and liabilities of the Participants as mentioned in this Byelaw are in addition to their rights and liabilities under these Bye Laws as Constituents, save where a specific provision of these Bye Laws or Regulations prescribed from time to time regarding any right or liability of a Participant is at variance with that applicable to a Constituent. In the event of such a variance, the specific provision by virtue of the terms and conditions of their registration with the Exchange, regarding any right or liability of a Participant shall prevail. (6) Rights and liabilities of the Participants shall be subject to these Bye Laws and Regulations as maybe prescribed by the relevant authority from time to time. 15 Confidential (7) Subject to the regulations prescribed from time to time, the relevant authority shall at any time be entitled to cancel the registration or recognition of a Participant on such terms and conditions as the relevant authority may specify. Save as otherwise expressly provided in the regulation or in the decision of the relevant authority, all rights and privileges available to the Participant shall accordingly stand terminated on such cancellation. (8) At the discretion of the Exchange, and subject to such regulations as may be prescribed or other terms and conditions as may be stipulated by the relevant authority, the Participant may be permitted conditional and / or limited access to the trading system or any part thereof, as may be decided by the relevant authority from time to time. 16 Confidential CHAPTER VII DEALINGS BY TRADING MEMBERS Jurisdiction (1) (a) Any deal entered into through automated trading system of the Exchange or any proposal for buying or selling or any acceptance of any such proposal for buying and selling shall be deemed to have been entered at the computerised processing unit of the Exchange at Mumbai and the place of contracting as between the trading members shall be at Mumbai. The trading members of the Exchange shall expressly record on their contract note that they have excluded the jurisdiction of all other Courts save and except, Civil Courts in Mumbai in relation to any dispute arising out of or in connection with or in relation to the contract notes, and that only the Civil Courts at Mumbai have exclusive jurisdiction in claims arising out of such dispute. The provisions of this Byelaw shall not object the jurisdiction of any court deciding any dispute as between trading members and their constituents to which the Exchange is not a part y. (b) The record of the Exchange as maintained by a central processing unit or a cluster of processing units or computer processing units, whether Maintained in any register, magnetic storage units, electronic storage optical storage units or computer storage units or in any other manner shall constitute the agreed and authentic record in relation to any transaction entered into through automated trading system. For the purposes of any dispute the record as maintained by the computer processing units by the Exchange shall constitute valid evidence in any dispute or claim between the constituents and the trading member of the Exchange or between the Trading members of the Exchange inter-se. Indemnity (2) The Exchange shall not be liable for any unauthorised dealings on the Exchange by any persons acting in the name of trading member(s). Trading Members Only Parties to Trades (3) (a) The Exchange does not recognise as parties to any deal any persons other than its own trading members, and (b) Every trading member is directly and wholly liable, in accordance with the Bye Laws, Rules and Regulations of the Exchange, to every other trading member with whom such trading member effects any deal on the Exchange for due fulfillment of the deal, whether such deal be for account of the trading member effecting it or for account of a constituent. All Dealings Subject to Bye Laws, Rules and Regulations (4) All dealings in securities on the Exchange shall be deemed made subject to the Bye Laws, Rules and Regulations of the Exchange and this shall be a part of the terms and conditions of all such deals and the deals shall be subject to the exercise by the relevant authority of the powers with respect thereto vested in it by the Bye Laws, Rules and Regulations of the Exchange. 17 Confidential Inviolability of Trade (5) (a) All the dealings in securities on the Exchange made subject to the Bye Laws, Rules and Regulations of the Exchange shall be in-violable and shall be cleared and settled in accordance with the B ye Laws, Rules and Regulations of the Exchange. However, the Exchange may by a notice annul the deal(s) on an application by a Trading Member in that behalf, if the relevant authority is satisfied after hearing the other part y/parties to the deal(s) that the deal(s) is/are fit for annulment on account of fraud or willful misrepresentation or material mistake in the trade. (b) Notwithstanding anything contained in clause (a) above, the Exchange may, to protect the interest of investors in securities and for proper regulation of the securities market, suo motu annul deal(s) at any time if the relevant authority is satisfied for reasons to be recorded in writing that such deal(s) is/are vitiated by fraud, material mistake, misrepresentation or market or price manipulation and the like. (c) Any annulment made pursuant to clauses (a) and (b) above, shall be final and binding upon the parties to trade(s). In such an event, the trading member shall be entitled to cancel the relevant contracts with its constituents. Deals by Representative trading members (6) (a) A trading member may authorise another trading member to act as a representative for a specified period with the prior permission of the relevant authority. (b) When a trading member employs another trading member as a representative to put through the transaction of a constituent, such representative shall report the transaction to the employing trading member at the same price as dealt in the market and the employing trading member shall report the same price to the constituent in respect of such transaction. Restriction on the trading members (7) Unless the Exchange otherwise specifies, a

Trading Member shall not become a constituent of another Trading Member. (8) Potential Default by Trading Member (1) The Exchange shall act in accordance with the circulars issued by SEBI from time to time with respect to Standard Operating Procedure in cases of Trading Member leading to default. (2) In accordance with the Circular(s) issued by SEBI under the above Byelaw, the Exchange shall issue instructions to the bank(s) concerned to freeze the bank account(s) maintained by a Trading Member, for all debits / withdrawal by the Trading Member in the event of potential default by such a Trading Member in meeting its obligations to a recognized stock exchange / Clearing Member / Clearing Corporation and / or repayment of funds / securities to his / its clients. 18 Confidential CHAPTER VIII TRADING SYSTEM AND MARKET MAKERS (1) Securities which will be eligible for market making, if at all, will be specified by the relevant authority from time to time. Registration of Market Makers (2) (a) Trading members may apply to be market makers in any security eligible for market making. (b) No trading member shall act as a market maker unless such Member is approved in accordance with this Bye Law and the approval has not been suspended or cancelled. Application for registration shall be in such and with such particulars as maybe prescribed from time to time. (c) A market maker shall apply to be registered to the relevant authority before commencing market making operations in each relevant security. If the relevant authority is satisfied, it shall within fifteen business days of receipt of such notification, designate the market maker as a registered market maker for that security. A registered market maker shall not commence to make a market in any relevant security until one business day after notice of its registration has been disseminated through the Trading system. (d) A registered market maker in any Exchange security must: (i) undertake to make bid and offer quotations in the trading system with respect to that security and to effect transactions in a minimum quantity of such other number of securities as may be prescribed from time to time at its quoted price per business day; (ii) undertake to make market for the security for as long as prescribed from time to time from the date the security becomes available for trading by public in the case of a registered market makers approved under Byelaw 2(b) above. (iii) undertake to execute orders for the purchase or sale of relevant securities at its quoted prices with trading members or clients. (e) A registered market maker may cease making a market in a particular Exchange security any time after a minimum period as prescribed from time to time from commencement of making market in that security, after having given the required notice of intention to the relevant authority. The required period of notice in this case shall be fifteen business days or such other period as maybe prescribed from time to time. (f) A registered market maker may cease making a market in that security provided formal approval has been obtained from t h e relevant authority. Such approval will normally be granted in situations where, in the opinion of the relevant authority, it is either impractical or undesirable for the registered market maker to continue to operate on account of events beyond its control. 19 Confidential (3) An obligation may be imposed on a trading member taking up market making operations in certain securities to take up additional market making operations in certain other securities as determined by the relevant authority from time to time. Suspension and Prohibition of Market Makers (4) (a) The relevant authority may limit or prohibit the authority of a registered market maker to display on or enter quotations into the trading system or deal in the securities in which he is registered as a market maker if: (i) such market maker has been or is expelled or suspended from membership of the Exchange, or is unable to comply with the Exchange's B ye Laws, Rules and Regulations or whose registration is cancelled by the Securities and Exchange Board of India; (ii) such market maker has defaulted on any transaction effected in respect of Exchange securities; (iii) such market maker is in such financial or operating difficulty that the relevant authority determines that such market maker cannot be permitted to display on or enter quotation into the trading system with safety to investors, creditors, other trading members of the Exchange; (iv) where such market maker in the view of the relevant authority, ceases to meet qualification requirements for registration as market maker. (b) Any market maker which the relevant authority takes action against pursuant to Byelaw 4 (a) above shall be notified in writing of such action. Such a market maker shall forthwith cease to make market. (c) Any market maker against which the relevant authority takes action may request an opportunity for a hearing within ten days of the date of notification pursuant to Byelaw 4 (b) above. A request for hearing shall not operate as a stay of action. (d) A written decision shall be issued within one week of the date of hearing and a copy shall be sent to the market maker. (e) On revocation of suspension or prohibition, the market maker can display on or enter quotations into the trading system. Operational Parameters for Market Makers (5) The relevant authority may determine and announce from time to time operational parameters for market makers which registered market makers shall adhere to.

(6) The operational parameters may, inter alia, include: (a) limit of spread between bid and offer rates for different securities, if found necessary; (b) fixation of market lots, odd lots and/or minimum number of securities to be offered to be bought or sold; 20 Confidential (c) limit of variation within a day or between days in bid and offer prices; (d) the minimum stock of scrips which the trading member must maintain, below which he must intimate the relevant authority; (e) in the event of stock of scrips with a market maker being sold out, allowing the market maker to quote only purchase price offers till such time as marketable lot of securities is built up to re-commence selling operations; and (f) other matters which may affect smooth operation of trading in securities in which he acts as a market maker, keeping in view larger interest of the public. 21 Confidential CHAPTER IX TRANSACTIONS AND SETTLEMENTS Transactions Business Hours (1) The business hours for dealing in the Exchange securities in different segments on the Exchange shall be during such time as may be decided by the relevant authority from time to time. The relevant authority may, from time to time, specify business hours for different types of deals such as for spot, ready and odd lots. (2) The relevant authority may declare a list of holidays in a calendar year. The relevant authority may from time to time alter or cancel any of the Exchange holidays fixed in accordance with these provisions. It may, for reasons to be recorded, close the market on days other than or in addition to holidays. Trading System (3) (a) Deals may be effected through order driven, quote driven (market makers) or such other system as the Exchange may put in place for the trading segments from time to time. (b) Deals between trading members may be effected by electronic media or computer

network or such other media as specified by the relevant authority from time to time. (c) Deals may be effected on spot, ready or on such other basis as may be specified by the relevant authority from time to time, subject to the Securities Contracts(Regulation) Act and Rules and the SEBI Act. Transaction at Best Quotation (4) In transaction with or on behalf of clients, trading members must indicate to the clients the current best quotation as reflected in the trading system. Operational Parameters for Trading (5) The relevant authority may determine and announce from time to time operational parameters regarding dealing of securities on the Exchange which trading members shall adhere to. (6) The operational parameters may, inter alia, include : (a) trading limits allowed which may include trading limits with reference to net worth and capital adequacy norms; (b) trading volumes and limits at which it will be incumbent for trading members to intimate the Exchange; (c) limit of spread between bid and offer rates for different securities, if found necessary; (d) fixation of market lots, odd lots and/or minimum number of securities to be offered to be bought or sold; 22 Confidential (e) limit of variation within a day or between days in bid and offer prices; (f) other matters which may affect smooth operation of trading in securities keeping in view larger interest of the public; (g) determine the types of trades permitted for a member and a security; (h) determining functional details of the trading system including the system design, users infrastructure, system operation. Suspension on Failure to meet Trading Limits (7) A trading member failing to restrict dealings on the Exchange to his trading limits as provided in these Bye Laws and Regulations shall be required by the relevant authority to reduce dealings to within trading limits forthwith. The relevant authority at its discretion may suspend a trading member for violation of trading limits and the suspension shall continue until the relevant authority withdraws such suspension. Contract Notes (8) Contract Notes shall be issued within such period as may be specified by the relevant authority from time to time for deals effected with clients or on behalf of clients, and will contain such details as the relevant authority may specify from time to time. The contract notes shall specify that the deal is subject to the B ye Laws, Rules and Regulations of the Exchange and subject to arbitration as provided therein. (9) Details of all deals effected, as may be specified, shall be communicated to the offices of the Exchange on the day of the transaction. (10) Unless otherwise provided in these Bye Laws, all dealings carried out in respect of Exchange securities shall be subject to the Bye Laws, Rules and Regulations of the Exchange. Delivery of securities (11) Delivery of all securities, documents and papers and payments in respect of all deals shall be in such manner and such place(s) as may be prescribed by the relevant authority from time to time. (12) The relevant authority shall specify from time to time, the securities, documents and papers which, when delivered in prescribed manner, shall constitute good delivery. Where circumstances so warrant, the relevant authority may determine, for reasons to be recorded, whether or not a delivery constitutes a good delivery and such finding shall be binding on the parties concerned. Where the relevant authority determines that a delivery does not constitute a good delivery, the delivering party shall be required to substitute good delivery instead within such time period as maybe specified. (13) The norms and procedures for delivery with respect to market lot, odd lot, minimum lot, part delivery, delivery of partly paid securities, etc. shall be as prescribed by the relevant authority from time to time. (14) The requirements and procedures for determining disputed deliveries or defective deliveries, and measures, procedures and system of resolving the dispute or defect in deliveries or of 23 Confidential consequences of such deliveries or the resolution shall, subject to these Bye Laws, be as prescribed by the relevant authority from time to time. Clearing and Settlement (15) Clearing and Settlement of deals shall be effected by the parties concerned by adopting and using such arrangements, systems, agencies or procedures as may be prescribed or specified by the relevant authority from time to time. Without prejudice to the generality of the foregoing, the relevant authority may prescribe or specify, for adoption and use by the trading members, participants, and other specified constituents, such custodial and depository services from time to time to facilitate smooth operation of the clearing and settlement arrangement or system. (16) The function of the clearing house may be performed by the Exchange or any agency identified by the relevant authority for this purpose. The role of the clearing house shall be to act as a facilitator for processing of deliveries and payments between trading members/ participants for trades effected by them on the Exchange. Settlement in each market segment of the Exchange shall be either on netted basis, gross basis, trade for trade basis or any other basis as may be specified by the relevant authority from time to time. Save as otherwise expressly provided in the regulations, when funds and securities are, under a prescribed arrangement, routed through the clearing house, the settlement responsibility shall rest wholly and solely upon the counter parties to the trade and /or the concerned trading members as the case may be and the clearing house shall act as the common agent of the trading members / Participants for receiving or giving delivery of securities and for receiving and paying funds, without incurring an y liability or obligation as a principal. Closing out (17) Subject to the regulations prescribed by the relevant authority from time to time, any dealing in securities made on the Exchange maybe closed out by buying in or selling out on the Exchange against a trading member and/or Participant as follows: - (a) in case of the selling trading member/Participant, on failure to complete delivery on the due date; and (b) in case of the buying trading member/Participant, on failure to pay the amount due on the due date, and any loss, damage or shortfall sustained or suffered as a result of such closing out shall be payable by the trading member or participant who failed to give due delivery or to pay amount due. (18) Closing out of contracts or dealings in securities and settlement of claims arising therefrom shall be in such manner within such time frame and subject to such conditions and procedures as may be prescribed from time to time by the relevant authority. (18A) Subject to the regulations prescribed by the relevant authority from time to time, any deal in securities made on the Exchange may be transferred from one Trading Member to another Trading Member under such circumstances and in respect of such trading segment of the Exchange as may be specified by the relevant authority from time to time. 24 Confidential Margins Margin Requirements (19) Dealings in any security or securities shall be subject to such margin requirements as the relevant authority may from time to time prescribe. Form of Margin Deposit (20) The margin to be furnished by a trading member under these Bye Laws and Regulations shall, inter alia, be in the form of cash or Deposit Receipt of or a Guarantee given by a Bank approved by the relevant authority or securities approved by it subject to such terms and conditions as it may from time to time impose. Deposits of cash shall not carry interest and the securities deposited by a trading member valued at the ruling market price shall exceed the margin amount for the time being covered by them by such percentage as relevant authority may from time to time specify. Value of Margin Deposit to be Maintained (21) The trading member depositing margin in the form of securities shall always maintain the value thereof at not less than the margin amount for the time being covered by them by providing further security to the satisfaction of the relevant authority which shall always determine the said value and whose valuation shall conclusively fix the amount of any deficiency to be made up from time to time Margin Deposit to be held by the Exchange (22) The margin deposits shall be held by the Exchange (and in case of Tri-party Repos, shall be held by the National Securities Clearing Corporation Limited ("NSCCL")) and when they are in the form of Bank Deposit Receipts and securities and such Receipts and securities may at the discretion of the relevant authority be transferred to such persons or to the name of a Bank approved by the Exchange. All margin deposits shall be held by the Exchange and/ or by the approved persons and /or by the approved Bank solely for and on account of the Exchange without any right whatsoever on the part of the depositing trading member or those in its right to call in question the exercise of such discretion. Letter of Declaration (23) A trading member depositing margin under the provisions of these Bye Laws and Regulations shall when required to do so sign a Letter of Declaration in respect of such matters and in such form or forms as the relevant authority may from time to time prescribe. Lien on Margins (24) The monies, Bank Deposit Receipts and other securities and assets deposited by a trading member by way of margin under the provisions of these Bye Laws and Regulations shall be subject to a first and paramount lien for any sum due to the Exchange. Subject to the above, the margin shall be available in preference to all other claims of the trading member for the due fulfillment of its engagements, obligations and liabilities arising out of or incidental to any bargains, dealings, transactions and contracts made subject to the Bye Laws, Rules and Regulations of the Exchange or anything done in pursuance thereof. 25 Confidential Evasion of Margin Requirements Forbidden (25) A trading member shall not directly or indirectly enter into any arrangement or adopt any procedure for the purpose of evading or assisting in the evasion of the margin requirements prescribed under these Bye Laws and Regulations. Suspension on Failure to Deposit Margin (26) A trading member failing to deposit margin as provided in these Bye Laws and Regulations shall be required by the relevant authority to suspend its business forthwith. A notice of such suspension shall be immediately placed on the trading system and the suspension shall continue until the margin required is duly deposited. Interest, Dividends, Rights and Calls (27) The buying constituent shall be entitled to receive all vouchers, coupons, dividends, cash bonus, bonus issues, rights and other privileges which may relate to securities bought cum voucher, cum coupons, cum dividends, cum cash bonus, cum bonus issues, cum rights, etc. The selling constituent shall be entitled to receive all vouchers, coupons, dividends, cash bonus, bonus issues, rights and other privileges which may relate to securities sold ex voucher, ex coupons, ex dividends, ex cash bonus, ex-bonus issues, ex rights, etc. (28) The manner, mode, information requirements, alterations, date and timing, etc., of adjustment with respect to vouchers, coupons, dividends, cash bonus, bonus issues, rights and other privileges between buying trading member and selling trading member shall be as prescribed by the relevant authority from time to time. The trading members shall be responsible between themselves and to their constituents for effecting such adjustments. (29) In respect of a contract in securities which shall become or are exchangeable for new or other securities under a scheme of reconstruction or reorganisation, the selling constituent shall deliver to the buyer, as the relevant authority directs, either the securities contracted for or the equivalent in securities and/or cash and/or other property receivable under such scheme of reconstruction or reorganisation. Brokerage on Dealings Brokerage (30) Trading members are entitled to charge brokerage upon the execution of all orders in respect of purchase or sale of securities at rates not exceeding the official scale prescribed by the relevant authority from time to time. Brokerage on Calls (31) A trading member buying securities on which calls have been prepaid by the seller may charge brokerage on the purchase price with the amount of such calls added. Underwriting Commission and Brokerage (32) Unless otherwise determined and restricted by the relevant authority, a trading member may, in its discretion, charge such brokerage or commission for underwriting or placing or acting as a broker or entering into any preliminary arrangement in respect of any floatation or new Issues 26 Confidential or Offer for Sale of any security as it may agree upon with the issuer or offerer or with the principal underwriters or brokers engaged by such issuer or offerer, subject to limits stipulated under the relevant statutory provisions as may be applicable from time to time. Sharing of Brokerage (33) (a) A trading member may not share brokerage with a person who - (i) is one for or with whom trading members are forbidden to do business under the Bye Laws, Rules and Regulations of the Exchange; (ii) is a trading member or employee in the employment of another trading member; (b) Irrespective of any arrangement for the sharing of brokerage with any person, the trading member shall be directly and wholly liable to every other member with whom such trading member effects any deal on the Exchange. 27 Confidential CHAPTER X RIGHTS AND LIABILITIES OF MEMBERS AND CONSTITUENTS All Contracts subject to Bye Laws, Rules and Regulations (1) All contracts relating to dealings permitted on the Exchange made by a trading member shall in all cases be deemed made subject to the Bye Laws, Rules and Regulations of the Exchange. This shall be a part of the terms and conditions of all such contracts and shall be subject to the exercise by the relevant authority of the powers with respect thereto vested in it by the B ye Laws, Rules and Regulations of the Exchange. Trading members not bound to accept Instructions and Orders (2) A trading member may not accept instructions or orders of constituents for purchase, sale, etc., of securities where circumstances appear to justify such action or on reasonable grounds. Where such refusal is made, the same may be communicated to the constituent. The trading member shall also furnish the constituent the reasons for such refusal on a request being made by him. Margin (3) A trading member shall have the right to demand from its constituent the margin deposit he has to provide under these Bye Laws, Rules and Regulations in respect of the business done by it for such constituent. A trading member shall also have the right to demand an initial margin in cash and/or securities from its constituent before executing an order and/or to stipulate that the constituent shall make a margin deposit or furnish additional margin according to changes in market prices. The constituent shall when from time to time called upon to do so forthwith provide a margin deposit and/or furnish additional margin as required under these Bye Laws, Rules and Regulations in respect of the business done for him by and/or as agreed upon by him with the trading member concerned. Closing-out of Constituent's Account (4) (a) The Exchange may close-out open positions of a constituent or transfer his open positions to another trading member under such circumstances and in respect of such trading segment of the Exchange as may be specified by the relevant authority from time to time. (b) When closing-out the account of a constituent a trading member may assume or take over such transactions to his own account as a principal at prices which are fair and justified by the condition of the market or he may close-out in the manner specified by the relevant authority and any expense incurred or any loss arising therefrom shall be borne by the constituent. The contract note in respect of such closing-out shall disclose whether the trading member is acting as a principal or on account of another constituent. (c) Notwithstanding anything contained in clause (a) above closing out of Participants' account shall be in such manner and subject to such stipulations as maybe prescribed from time to time. Trading member not Liable to attend to Registration of Transfer 28 Confidential (5) A trading member shall not be deemed to be under any obligation to attend to the transfer of securities and the registration thereof in the name of the constituent. If it attends to such work in the ordinary course or at the request or desire or by the consent of the constituent it shall be deemed to be the agent of the constituent in the matter and shall not be responsible for loss in transit or for the issuer's refusal to transfer nor be under any other liability or obligation other than that specifically imposed by these B ye Laws, Rules and Regulations. The stamp duty, the transfer fees and other charges payable to the issuer, the fee for attending to the registration of securities and all incidental expenses such as postage incurred by the trading member shall be borne by the constituent Registration of Securities when in Name of trading member or Nominee (6) (a) When the time available to the constituents of a trading member is less than thirty days to complete transfers and lodge the securities for registration before the closing of the transfer books and where the security is purchased cum interest, dividend, bonus or rights which the issuer may have announced or declared the trading member may register the securities in its or its nominee's name and recover the transfer fee, stamp duty and other charges from the buying constituent. (b) The trading member shall give immediate intimation to the Exchange of the names of such constituents and details of the transactions as may be specified by the relevant authority from time to time. The trading member shall also give immediate intimation thereof to the buying constituent and shall stand indemnified for the consequences of any delay in delivery caused by such action. (c) The trading member shall be obliged to retransfer the security in the name of the original constituent as soon as it has become ex interest, dividend, bonus or rights. Closing-out/ transfer by Constituent on Failure to perform a Contract (7) If a trading member fails to complete the performance of a contract by delivery or payment in accordance with the provisions of these Bye Laws, Rules and Regulations the constituent shall, after giving notice in writing to the trading member and Exchange, close-out such contract through any other trading member of the Exchange or make an application to the Exchange for transfer of contracts to another trading member as soon as possible and any loss or damages sustained as a result of such closing-out or transfer, as the case may be, shall be immediately payable by the defaulting trading member to the constituent. If closing-out or transfer be not effected as provided herein, the damages between the parties shall be determined on such basis as specified by the relevant authority from time to time and the constituent and the trading member shall forfeit all further right of recourse against each other. No Lien on Constituent's Securities (8)If a trading member is declared a defaulter after delivering securities on account of his constituent, the constituent shall be entitled to claim and on offering proof considered satisfactory by the relevant authority, and in the absolute discretion of the relevant authority, receive from the Exchange accordingly as the relevant authority directs either such securities or the value thereof subject to payment or deduction of the amount if any due by him to the defaulter. Complaint by Constituent 29 Confidential (9) When a complaint has been lodged by a constituent with the relevant authority that any trading member has failed to implement his dealings, the relevant authority shall investigate the complaint and if it is satisfied that the complaint is justified it may take such disciplinary actionas it deems fit. Relationship between trading member and Constituents (10) Without prejudice to any other law for the time being in force and subject to these Bye Laws, the mutual rights and obligations inter se between the trading member and his/its constituent shall be such as may be prescribed by the relevant authority from time to time. (11) The Relevant Authority shall constitute an Investors' Services Committee to supervise the working of the Investors' Services Cell of the Exchange and in suitable cases attend to grievances of the Investors personally. The composition of Investors' Services Committee shall be such as may be prescribed by SEBI. 30 Confidential CHAPTER XI ARBITRATION Definitions 'Arbitrator' shall mean a sole arbitrator or a panel of arbitrators. 'Act' shall mean the Arbitration and Conciliation Act, 1996 and includes any statutory modification, replacement or re-enactment thereof, for the time being in force. 'Admissible claim value' shall mean the claim value admissible to the Constituent as ascertained by the Grievance Redressal Committee or Panel and recorded in the directions or order. 'Arbitral Award' shall mean an award passed by the Arbitrator. 'Appellate Arbitrator' shall mean a panel of arbitrators who hears the appeal filed against the Arbitral Award. 'Appellate Arbitral Award' shall mean an award passed by the Appellate Arbitrator. Reference to Arbitration (1) All claims, differences or disputes between the Trading Members inter se and between Trading Members and Constituents arising out of or in relation to dealings, contracts and transactions made subject to the Bye-Laws, Rules and Regulations of the Exchange or with reference to anything incidental thereto or in pursuance thereof or relating to their validity, construction, interpretation, fulfilment or the rights, obligations and liabilities of the parties thereto and including any question of whether such dealings, transactions and contracts have been entered into shall be submitted to arbitration in accordance with the provisions of these Byelaws and Regulations. The Exchange shall be entitled to facilitate arbitration for such disputes and parties as mentioned in the provisions of Byelaw 1, including the arbitration reference filed by Trading Member against the directions or order of the Grievance Redressal Committee GRC), by adopting such procedures as may be prescribed by it under this Chapter. (1A) All claims, differences or disputes between the Trading Members and authorised persons and between authorised persons and Clients of authorised persons arising out of or in relation to dealings, contracts and transactions made subject to the Byelaws, Rules and Regulations of the Exchange or with reference to anything incidental thereto or in pursuance thereof or relating to their validity, construction, interpretation, fulfilment or the rights, obligations and liabilities of the parties thereto and including any question of whether such dealings, transactions and contracts have been entered into shall be submitted to arbitration in accordance with the provisions of these Byelaws and Regulations; Provided in disputes between authorised persons and clients of authorised persons, the Trading Member should be added as a necessary party. (1B) All claims, differences or disputes between the Trading Members inter se, Trading Members and Constituents, whether or not registered as Participants, Constituents inter se, whether or not registered as Participants, arising out of or in relation to dealings, contracts and transactions 31 Confidential executed or reported on the Wholesale Debt Market Trading Segment of the Exchange and made subject to the Byelaws, Rules and Regulations of the Exchange or with reference to anything incidental thereto or in pursuance thereof or relating to their validity, construction, interpretation, fulfillment or the rights, obligations and liabilities of the parties thereto and including any question of whether such dealings, transactions and contracts have been entered into shall be submitted to arbitration in accordance with the provisions of these Byelaws and Regulations. Provided this Byelaw shall not in any way affect the jurisdiction of the Exchange on the Trading Member, through whom such a Participant has dealt with or traded, in regard thereto and such Trading Member shall continue to remain responsible, accountable and liable to the Exchange in this behalf. (1C) All claims, differences or disputes arising between an Issuer and a Constituent in respect of such matters as may be specifically provided from time to time in the Listing Agreement as entered into by an Issuer with the Exchange shall be submitted to arbitration in accordance with the provisions of these Byelaws and Regulations. For the purpose of these Byelaws and Regulations, the term 'Issuer' shall have the same meaning as defined in these Byelaws and the term 'Constituent' shall mean the investor who has bought or sold, on the Exchange, the securities of the Issuer in respect of which the claim, differences or dispute has arisen. (1D) The Exchange shall be entitled to facilitate arbitration for such disputes and parties other than those mentioned in the provisions of Byelaws 1, (1A), (1B), and (1C) of this Chapter by adopting such procedures as may be prescribed by it under this Chapter. Provisions of these Byelaws and Regulations deemed to form part of all dealings, contracts and transactions (2) In all dealings, contracts and transactions, which are made or deemed to be made subject to the Byelaws, Rules and Regulations of the Exchange, the provisions relating to arbitration as provided in these Byelaws and Regulations shall form and shall be deemed to form part of the dealings, contracts and transactions and the parties shall be deemed to have entered into an arbitration agreement in writing by which all claims, differences or disputes of the nature referred to in B ye laws (1), (1A), (1B) and (1C) above shall be submitted to arbitration as per the provisions of these Byelaws and Regulations. Limitation period for arbitration (3) The limitation period for filing an arbitration application shall be governed by the law of limitation i.e. The Limitation Act, 1963 as specified under section 43 of the Act. Explanation: Arbitration Applications filed prior to September 1, 2010, where the Arbitration application has been dismissed solely on grounds of limitations and three years from the date of dispute have not yet elapsed will be covered in the limitation period stated above. Power of the Relevant Authority to prescribe Regulations (4) (a) The Relevant Authority may, from time to time prescribe Regulations for the following: 32 Confidential (i) The procedure to be followed by the parties in arbitral proceedings. In particular, and without prejudice to the generality of the foregoing power, such procedure ma y, inter alia, provide for the following: (a) the forms to be used; (b) the fees to be paid; (c) the mode, manner and time period for submission of all pleadings by both the parties; (d) matters relating to requests from the parties for amending or supplementing the pleadings; and (e) the consequences upon failure to submit such pleadings by the parties. (ii) The procedure to be followed by the arbitrator in conducting the arbitral proceedings. In particular, and without prejudice to the generality of the foregoing power, such procedure ma y, inter alia, provide for (a) Adjournment of hearings; and (b) terms and conditions subject to which the arbitrator may appoint experts to report on specific issues and the procedure to be followed in arbitral proceedings upon such an appointment. (iii) Different set of arbitration procedures for different claims, differences or disputes after taking into consideration such circumstances and facts as the Relevant Authority may deem fit, which circumstances and facts may include the value of the subject matter and the persons who are involved as parties to such claims, differences or disputes. (iv) Creation of seats of arbitration for different regions or prescribing geographical locations for conducting arbitrations and prescribing the courts which shall have jurisdiction for the purpose of the Act. (v) The claims, differences or disputes which may be referred to a sole arbitrator and the claims, differences or disputes which may be referred to a panel of arbitrators. (vi) The procedure for selection of persons eligible to act as arbitrators. (vii) The procedure for appointment of arbitrator. (viii) The terms, conditions and qualifications subject to which any arbitrator may be appointed. (ix) Determination of the number of arbitrators in the case of a panel of arbitrators, subject to the condition that where any claim, difference or dispute is heard and determined by Panel of Arbitrators, the number of arbitrators of such a panel shall not be an even number and shall not include Trading Members. 33 Confidential (x) The time period within which a substitute arbitrator has to be appointed in case the office of the arbitrator falls vacant for any reason whatsoever. (xi) The matters to be disclosed by any person who is approached in connection with his possible appointment as an arbitrator. (xii) The procedure to be adopted by the parties for challenging an arbitrator. (xiii) (a) The claims, differences or disputes which, may be decided by the arbitrator without a hearing unless either party in writing requests the Relevant Authority for a hearing and the time period within which such a request shall be made. (b) The claims, differences or disputes which, may be decided by the arbitrator only by hearing the parties unless both the parties jointly waive the right to such hearing and the time period within which such a waiver shall be made. (xiv) The place of arbitration for each reference and the places where the arbitrator can meet for consultation, for hearing witnesses, experts, or the parties, or for inspection of documents, goods or other property. (xv) The making of the arbitral award including the manner in which a decision is to be taken in the case of panel of arbitrators and the form and contents of the arbitral award. The term arbitral award shall also include an arbitral award on agreed terms. Prescriptions as to the contents of the arbitral award may include provisions for costs and where the arbitral award is for the payment of money, may include interest payable on principal sum due. (xvi) The amount of deposit or supplementary deposit, as the case may be, as an advance for the costs which it expects will be incurred in respect of the claim, difference or dispute; Provided where a counter-claim is submitted to the arbitrator, a separate amount of deposit for the counter-claim may also be prescribed. (xvii) The administrative assistance which the Exchange may render in order to facilitate the conduct of arbitral proceedings. (xviii) All matters regarding the mode and the manner of service of notices and communications by the parties including communication addressed to arbitrator. (xix) Any other matter which in the opinion of the Relevant Authority is required to be dealt with in the Regulations to facilitate arbitration. (b) The Relevant Authority from time to time may amend, modify, alter, repeal, or add to the provisions of the Regulations. 34 Confidential Disclosure by persons to be appointed as arbitrators (5) Every person who is approached in connection with his possible appointment as an arbitrator, shall disclose to the Relevant Authority in writing any circumstances likely to give rise to justifiable doubts as to his independence and impartiality. If the person discloses any circumstances which in the opinion of the Relevant Authority are likely to give rise to justifiable doubts as to his independence and impartiality, then he shall not be appointed as an arbitrator. Disclosure by persons appointed as arbitrators (6) An arbitrator, from the time of his appointment and throughout the arbitral proceedings, shall, without delay, disclose to the Relevant Authority in writing any circumstances referred to in Byelaw (5) above which have come to his knowledge after his appointment as an arbitrator. Termination of mandate of the arbitrator (7) The mandate of the arbitrator shall terminate if (a) the arbitrator withdraws from office for any reason; or (b) in the opinion of the Relevant Authority, the arbitrator becomes de jure or de facto unable to perform his functions or for other reasons fails to act without undue delay including failure to make the arbitral award within the time period prescribed by the Relevant Authority. Such a decision of the Relevant Authority shall be final and binding on the parties; or (c) the mandate of the arbitrator is terminated by the Relevant Authority upon receipt of written request for the termination of the mandate of the arbitrator from both the parties to arbitration; or (d) the arbitrator discloses any circumstances referred to in Byelaws (5) and (6) which in the opinion of the Relevant Authority are likely to give rise to justifiable doubts as to his independence and impartiality. (e) the arbitral proceedings are terminated as provided for herein. Supplying of vacancy to the office of the arbitrator (8) At any time before the making of the arbitral award should the office of the arbitrator fall vacant for any reason whatsoever including any vacancy due to the illness or death of the arbitrator or termination of the mandate of the arbitrator by the Relevant Authority or otherwise, the vacancy shall be supplied by the Relevant Authority by following the same procedure as specified by it for appointment of the arbitrator. Consideration of recorded proceedings and evidence (9) Unless otherwise agreed by parties, any arbitrator who has been appointed by the Relevant Authority to supply a vacancy to the office of the arbitrator, may repeat any hearings previously held. 35 Confidential Order or ruling of previous arbitrator not invalid. (10) An order or ruling of the arbitrator made prior to the termination of his mandate shall not be invalid solely because his mandate has been terminated; Provided that when the termination has been effected pursuant to Byelaw (7)(d), the order or ruling of the arbitrator made prior to termination of his mandate shall become invalid unless otherwise agreed upon by the parties. Interim arbitral award and interim measures ordered by the arbitrator (11) The arbitrator may be empowered to make an interim arbitral award as well as to provide interim measures of protection. An arbitrator may require a party to provide appropriate security in connection with an interim measure. Appearance in arbitral proceedings by counsel, attorney or advocate (12) In arbitral proceedings where both the parties are Trading Members, the parties shall not be permitted to appear by counsel, attorney or advocate but where one of the parties is a Constituent, then the Constituent shall be permitted to appear by counsel, attorney or advocate. If the Constituent chooses to appear by counsel, attorney or advocate, then the Trading Member and Issuer shall be granted a similar privilege. (13) (a) Adjournment Adjournment, if an y, shall be granted by the arbitrator only in exceptional cases, for bona fide reasons to be recorded in writing. (b) Time for completion of Arbitration The arbitral proceedings shall be concluded by way of issue of Arbitral Award within four months from the date of appointment Arbitrator(s) and may be extended by such further time periods may be specified by the Managing Director. (13A) (i) In cases where the Trading Member informs the exchange of his intention to pursue arbitration against the Order of GRC in favour of the Constituent, within 7 days from the date of signing of GRC Order, and the admissible claim value is not more than Rupees Twenty Lakhs then 50% of the admissible claim value or Rs. 2.00 Lakhs, whichever is less, shall be released to the Constituent from Investor Protection Fund (IPF) of the Exchange. (ii) In case the arbitration award is in favour of the Constituent in the matter as mentioned in Clause (i) above or Arbitration Award passed in favour of the Constituent is not more than Rupees Twenty Lakhs in the matter directly filed for arbitration and the member conveys his intention of preferring appeal against such arbitral award within 7 days from the date of receipt of the award, then 50% of the award amount or Rs. 3.00 lakhs, whichever is less will be released to the constituent from IPF of the Exchange. The amount released shall exclude the amount already released to the constituent at clause (i) above. (iii) In case the appellate arbitration award is in favour of the constituent and the trading member conveys his intention of filing petition in court to set aside the Appellate arbitration award u/s 34 of the Arbitration and Conciliation Act, 1996 within 7 days from the receipt of the Appellate Arbitration Award, then 75% of the amount determined in the appellate arbitration award or Rs. 5.00 lakhs (Rs. Five Lakhs), whichever is less will be released to the Constituent from IPF 36 Confidential of the Exchange. The amount released shall exclude the amount already released to the constituent at clause (i) and (ii) above. (iv) Before release of the said amounts from the IPF to the Constituent, the Exchange shall obtain appropriate undertaking or indemnity from the Constituent against the release of the amount from IPF, to ensure return of the amount so released to the Constituent, in case the proceedings are decided against the Constituent. (v) If it is observed that there is an attempt by Constituent either individually or through collusion with Trading Member(s) or with any other stakeholders, to misuse the clauses (i) to (iv) above, then without prejudice to the powers of SEBI to take action, appropriate action in this regard shall be taken against any such person, by the Relevant Authority, including disqualification of the person so involved from henceforth accessing the benefits of these provisions. (vi) The amount released to the Constituent from IPF as per the admissible claim will be replenished back to IPF from the deposit or collaterals or any other amounts, including the blocked amount of the Trading Member available with the Exchange/National Securities Clearing Corporation Limited (NSCCL) and the balance will be paid to the Constituent in the following cases: (a) The Trading Member informs the Exchange, within 7 days from the date of signing of GRC directions ascertaining the admissible claim amount, his intention to refer the matter to arbitration and fails to refer the matter to arbitration within the prescribed time limit i.e. three years. (b) The Trading Member fails to inform the Exchange his intention to prefer an appeal before Appellate Arbitrators of the Exchange or court or intention to make a request u/s 33 of Arbitration and Conciliation Act, 1996 for rectification or correction of award, against the arbitral award, within 7 days from the date of receipt of award. (c) The Trading Member informs the Exchange his intention to prefer an appeal before Appellate Arbitrators of the Exchange or court but fails to prefer the same within prescribed time limit (one month from date of receipt of award in case of appellate arbitration and three months from date of receipt of award, in case of petition in court). For cases where request is made under Section 33 of Arbitration and Conciliation Act, 1996 for clarification or rectification of award, the one month period in case of appeal and three months period in case of petition mentioned above will be from the date of receipt of the order passed by arbitrator u/s 33 applications by the Trading Member. (d) The matter is decided in favour of the Constituent after conclusion of arbitration or appellate arbitration or court proceedings and the Trading Member decides not to pursue the matter further. (vii)(a) In case Constituent loses at any stage of the proceedings and decides not to pursue the matter further, then the Constituent shall refund the amount released from IPF, back to the IPF of the Exchange. In case the Constituent fails to make good the amount released 37 Confidential out of IPF then the Constituent (based on the PAN of the Constituent) shall not be allowed to trade on any of the Exchanges till such time the Constituent refunds the amount to IPF. Further the securities lying in the demat account(s) of the Constituent shall be frozen till such time as the Constituent refunds the amount to the IPF. (vii)(b) In addition to the above, the constituent may also be declared as a defaulter if the constituent does not pay the award amount to the trading member as directed in the

GRC/arbitration/appellate arbitration order and also does not appeal at the next level of redressal mechanism within the timelines prescribed by SEBI or file an application to court to set aside such order in accordance with section 34 of the Arbitration and Conciliation Act, 1996 (in case aggrieved by arbitration or appellate award). The common database of such clients shall be accessible to members/ depository participants across the stock exchanges/ depositories. (viii) The Exchange may be empowered to initiate any proceedings in a court of law for the purpose of recovering any amounts due to the IPF, against such Constituent who fails to make good the amount released to him out of IPF as mentioned in clause (vii) above. (13B) For cases, other than cases falling under the purview of Byelaw 13A above, where the arbitration award is passed against the Trading Member and/or its authorised persons and in favour of a Constituent, the Exchange may debit from the deposits or other monies of the Trading Member lying with the Exchange, the amount of award payable to the awardee together with interest payable, if any, till the date of debit after setting off the counter claim of the Trading Member and/or its s authorised persons allowed under the award, if any, and keep aside the said amount in a separate account to be dealt with in such manner as mentioned in Byelaw 13C below; Provided however, where the award is for the delivery of securities, the Exchange may consider the closing price of such securities on the Exchange as on the date of the award or such other date the relevant authority may specify to be reasonable, stating reasons for arriving at the value of such securities and award amount. (13C) (a) The Exchange shall make the payment of the Arbitral Award amount kept aside in a separate account as specified in Byelaw 13B above to the awardee, along with interest earned on the amount that has been set aside, in case the Trading member fails to convey within 7 days of receipt of the award his desire to challenge the award or appellate award in court to the Exchange. Further, the Exchange shall release the award amount as soon as the time for preferring an appeal before the Appellate Arbitrator or Court has expired and no appeal has been preferred. (b) The Exchange shall make payment of the Appellate Arbitral Award to the awardee along with the interest earned on the amount that has been set aside as soon as i) the time for making an application to a court to set aside such Appellate Arbitral Award under Section 34 of Act has expired and no application has been made, or ii) an application to a court to set aside such Appellate Arbitral Award under Section 34 of the Act, having been made, has been refused by such court, or 38 Confidential iii) an application to a court to set aside such Appellate Arbitral Award under Section 34 of the Act, having been made, but where no stay has been granted by such court within a period of three months from the date on which the party making that application had received the Appellate Arbitral Award. Arbitration proceedings subject to the provisions of the Act (14) The arbitration proceedings as provided for by the provisions of these Byelaws and Regulations shall be subject to the provisions of the Act to the extent not provided for in these Byelaws or the Regulations. Construction of references (15) For the purposes of section 2(6) of the Act, in all claims, differences or disputes which are required to be submitted to arbitration as per the provisions of these Byelaws and the Regulations, wherever Part 1 of the Act leaves the parties free to determine a certain issue, the parties shall be deemed to have authorised the Relevant Authority to determine that issue. Administrative assistance (16) For the purpose of section 6 of the Act, in all claims, differences or disputes which are required to be submitted to arbitration as per the provisions of these Byelaws and Regulations, the parties shall be deemed to have arranged for administrative assistance of the Relevant Authority in order to facilitate the conduct of the arbitral proceedings. Jurisdiction (17) The arbitration and appellate arbitration shall be conducted at the regional centre nearest to the address provided by Constituent in the KYC form or as per the change in address communicated thereafter by the Constituent to the trading member. Further, in case the award amount is more than Rs. 50 Lakh, the next level of proceedings (arbitration and appellate arbitration) may take place at the nearest metro city, if desired by any of the party involved. The additional cost for arbitration and appellate arbitration, if any, is to be borne by the appealing party. Furthermore, the application under Section 34 of the Act, if any, against the decision of the Appellate Arbitral Award passed by the Appellate Arbitrator shall be filed in the competent court nearest to the address provided by Constituent in the KYC form or as per the change in address communicated thereafter by the Constituent to the trading member. . Exclusion (18) For removal of doubts, it is hereby clarified that the Exchange shall not be construed to be a party to the dealings, contracts and transactions referred to under these Byelaws; and the provisions of this Chapter shall not apply in case of claims, differences or disputes between the Exchange and a Trading Member and no arbitration shall lie between the Exchange and a Trading Member. Appellate Arbitration (19) (a) A party aggrieved by an Arbitral Award may appeal to the Appellate Arbitrator against Arbitral Award within one month from the date of receipt of Arbitral Award and in 39 Confidential such manner as prescribed by the Relevant Authority from time to time notwithstanding the provisions contained under Byelaw 3. (b) The Appellate Arbitrator shall consist of three arbitrators who shall be different from the ones who passed the Arbitral Award appealed against and such Appellate Arbitrators shall dispose of the appeal by way of issue of an Appellate Arbitral Award within three months from the date of appointment of the Appellate Arbitrator. (c) A party aggrieved by the Appellate Arbitral Award may file an application in accordance with Section 34 of the Act before the court of competent jurisdiction nearest to the address provided by Constituent in the KYC form or as per the change in address communicated thereafter by the Constituent to the trading member. (d) The above provisions of Byelaws 1 to 18 shall be applicable to Appellate Arbitration. 40 Confidential CHAPTER XII DEFAULT Declaration of Default (1) A trading member may be declared a defaulter by direction / circular / notification of the relevant authority of the trading segment if- (a) he is unable to fulfill his obligations; or (b) he admits or discloses his inability to fulfill or discharge his duties, obligations and liabilities; or (c) he fails or is unable to pay within the specified time the damages and the money difference due on a closing-out effected against him under these Bye Laws, Rules and Regulations; or (d) he fails to pay any sum due to the Exchange or to submit or deliver to the Exchange on the due date, delivery and receive orders, statement of differences and securities, balance sheet and such other clearing forms and other statements as the relevant authority may from time to time prescribe; or (e) if he fails to pay or deliver to the Defaulters‘ Committee all monies, securities and other assets due to a trading member who has been declared a defaulter within such time of the declaration of default of such trading member as the relevant authority may direct; or (f) if he fails to abide by the arbitration proceedings as laid down under the Bye Laws, Rules and Regulations; or (g) if he, being an individual and /or partnership firm, /it, being a company incorporated under the Companies Act, files an application a petition before a Court of Law for adjudication of himself as an insolvent or an insolvency application is filed against it in accordance with the provisions of the Insolvency and Bankruptcy Code 2016 or any other analogous bankruptcy laws applicable to him / it, as the case maybe. (1A) Without prejudice to the foregoing, if a trading member is either expelled or declared a defaulter by any other recognised stock exchange on which he is a member or if the registration certificate is cancelled by SEBI, the said Trading Member may be expelled from the Exchange after providing an opportunity of being heard to such Trading Member. Notwithstanding anything contained in this Byelaw, the trading facility of the member shall be withdrawn immediately after the receipt of information of expulsion /default by any other stock exchange or cancellation of registration certificate by SEBI. Failure to fulfil Obligations (2) The relevant authority may order a trading member to be declared a defaulter if he fails to meet an obligation to a trading member or constituent arising out of Exchange transactions. 41 Confidential Insolvent a Defaulter(3) A trading member, being an individual and/or partnership firm, /it, being a company incorporated under the Companies Act, an application is admitted against him/ it in accordance with the provisions of the Insolvency and Bankruptcy Code 2016 or any other analogous bankruptcy laws applicable to him / it, as the case maybe, shall be declared a defaulter although he/it may not have at the same time defaulted on any of his / its obligations on the Exchange provided however the time for preferring an appeal against such order under the applicable Acts, if any, has expired. Trading member's Duty to Inform (4) A trading member shall be bound to notify the Exchange immediately if there be a failure by any trading member to discharge his liabilities in full. Compromise Forbidden (5) A trading member guilty of accepting from any trading member anything less than a full and bona fide money payment in settlement of a debt arising out of a transaction in securities shall be suspended for such period as the relevant authority may determine. Notice of Declaration of Default (6) On a trading member being declared a defaulter a notice to that effect shall be placed forthwith on the trading system of the relevant trading segment. Defaulter's Book and Documents (7) When a trading member has been declared a defaulter, the Defaulters' Committee shall take charge of all his books of accounts, documents, papers and vouchers to ascertain the state of his affairs and the defaulter shall hand over such books, documents, papers and vouchers to the Defaulters' Committee. List of Debtors and Creditors (8) The defaulter shall file with the Defaulters' Committee within such time of the declaration of his default as the relevant authority may direct a written statement containing a complete list of his debtors and creditors and the sum owing by and to each. Defaulter to give Information (9) The defaulter shall submit to the Defaulters' Committee such statement of accounts, information and particulars of his affairs as the Defaulters' Committee may from time to time require and if so desired shall appear before the Committee at its meetings held in connection with its default. Inquiry (10) The Defaulters' Committee shall enter into a strict inquiry into the accounts and dealings of the defaulter in the market and shall report to the relevant authority anything improper, unbusiness like or unbecoming a trading member in connection therewith which may come to its knowledge. Vesting of assets in the Exchange 42 Confidential (11) The Defaulters' Committee shall call in and realise the security deposits in any form, margin money, other amounts lying to the credit of and securities deposited by the defaulter and recover all moneys, securities and other assets due, payable or deliverable to the defaulter by any other Trading Member in respect of any transaction or dealing made subject to the B ye-laws, Rules and Regulations of the Exchange and such assets shall vest ipso facto, on declaration of any trading member as a defaulter, in the Exchange for the benefit of and on account of any dues of the Exchange, National Securities Clearing Corporation Limited, Securities and Exchange Board of India, other trading members, Constituents and registered authorised persons of the defaulter, approved banks and any other persons as may be approved by the Defaulters' Committee and other recognised stock exchanges. Payment to Defaulters' Committee (12) (a) All monies, securities and other assets due, payable or deliverable to the defaulter must be paid or delivered to the Defaulters' Committee within such time of the declaration of default as the relevant authority may direct. A trading member violating this provision shall be declared a defaulter. (b) A trading member who shall have received a difference on account or shall have received any consideration in any transaction prior to the date fixed for settling such account or transaction shall, in the event of the trading member from whom he received such difference or consideration being declared a defaulter, refund the same to the Defaulters' Committee for the benefit and on account of the creditor members. Any trading member who shall have paid or given such difference or consideration to any other trading member prior to such settlement day shall again pay or give the same to the Defaulters' Committee for the benefit and on account of the creditor member in the event of the default of such other member. (c) A trading member who receives from another trading member during any clearing a claim note or credit note representing a sum other than a difference due to him or due to his constituent which amount is to be received by him on behalf and for the account of that constituent shall refund such sum if such other trading member be declared a defaulter within such number of days as prescribed by the relevant authority after the settling da y. Such refunds shall be made to the Defaulters' Committee for the benefit and on account of the creditor members and it shall be applied in liquidation of the claims of such creditor members whose claims are admitted in accordance with these Bye Laws, Rules and Regulations. Distribution (13) The Defaulters' Committee shall at the risk and cost of the creditor members pay all assets received in the course of realisation into such bank and/or keep them with the Exchange in such names as the relevant authority may from time to time direct and shall distribute the same as soon as possible pro rata but without interest among creditor members whose claims are admitted in accordance with these B ye Laws, Rules and Regulations. Closing-out (14) (a) Trading members having open transactions with the defaulter shall close out such transactions on the Exchange after declaration of default. Such closing out shall be in such manner as may be prescribed by the relevant authority from time to time. Subject 43 Confidential to the regulations in this regard prescribed by the relevant authority, when in the opinion of the relevant authority, circumstances so warrant, such closing out shall be deemed to have taken place in such manner as may be determined by the relevant authority or other authorised persons of the Exchange. (b) Differences arising from the above adjustments of closing out shall be claimed from the defaulter or paid to the Defaulters' Committee for the benefit of creditor trading members of the defaulter. (15) [Deleted] (16) [Deleted] (17) [Deleted] (18) [Deleted] Accounts of Defaulters' Committee (19) The Defaulters' Committee shall keep a separate account in respect of all monies, securities and other assets payable to a defaulter which are received by him and shall defray therefrom all costs, charges and expenses incurred in or about the collection of such assets or in or about any proceedings it takes in connection with the default. Report (20) The Defaulters' Committee shall every six months present a report to the relevant authority relating to the affairs of a defaulter and shall show the assets realised, the liabilities discharged and dividends given. Inspection of Accounts (21) All accounts kept by the Defaulters' Committee in accordance with these B yeLaws, Rules and Regulations shall be open to inspection by any creditor trading member. Scale of Charges (22) The charges to be paid to the Exchange on the amounts transferred to the Defaulters' Committee account shall be such sum as the relevant authority may from time to time prescribe. Application of Assets (23) The Defaulters' Committee shall apply the net assets remaining in its hands after defraying all such costs, charges and expenses as are allowed under the Rules, Bye- laws and Regulations to be incurred by the

Exchange, in satisfying the claims in the order of priority provided hereunder:- (a) Dues to the Exchange, National Securities Clearing Corporation Limited, Securities and Exchange Board of India 44 Confidential The payment of such subscriptions, debts, fines, fees, charges and other moneys due to the Exchange, National Securities Clearing Corporation Limited, Securities and Exchange Board of India, in the order in which their names appear herein; (b) Dues to other Trading Members and to Constituents and registered sub- brokers of the defaulter The payments as may be admitted by the Defaulters' Committee, as being due to other Trading Members and Constituents and registered sub- brokers of the defaulter for debts, liabilities, obligations and claims arising out of any contracts made by the defaulter subject to the Rules, Bye-laws and Regulations of the Exchange, shall, if the amount is insufficient, be distributed pro rata amongst other Trading Members, all the Constituents and registered sub- brokers of the defaulter. The other Trading members in turn share the amounts so received with their Constituents on pro rata basis. (c) Dues to the Approved Banks and claims of any other persons as approved by the Defaulters' Committee After making payments under Clause (b) above, the amounts remaining, if any, shall be utilised to meet the claims of the approved banks and of any other person as may be admitted by the Defaulters' Committee. The claims of the approved banks should have arisen by virtue of the Exchange or National Securities Clearing Corporation Limited invoking any bank guarantee issued by the bank concerned to the Exchange or National Securities Clearing Corporation Limited as the case may be on behalf of the defaulter to fulfil his obligation of submitting bank guarantee, guaranteeing discharge of obligations under the

Byelaws, Rules and Regulations of NSEIL/NSCCL. The claims of other persons should have arisen out of or incidental to the transaction done on the Exchange or requirements laid down by the Exchange, provided that if the amount available be insufficient to pay all such claims in full, they shall be paid pro rata, and (d) Dues to any other recognised stock exchange: After meeting the claims under (c) above, the remaining amounts, if any, shall be disbursed to any other recognised Stock Exchange for the purpose of meeting the obligations of the defaulter as a member of that Exchange. If the defaulter is a member of more than one recognised stock exchange, then the remaining amounts shall be distributed amongst all such recognised stock exchanges and if the remaining amount is insufficient to meet the claims of all such stock exchanges, then the remaining amount shall be distributed pro rata among all such stock exchanges. (e) Surplus assets: Surplus assets, if any, may be released to the defaulter after a period of atleast one year from the date of declaration of the trading member as defaulter or after satisfying the claims falling under Bye-law 23, whichever is later. Certain claims not to be entertained (24) The Defaulters‘ Committee shall not entertain any claim against a defaulter: 45 Confidential (a) which arises out of a contract in securities dealings in which are not permitted or which are not made subject to B ye Laws, Rules and Regulations of the Exchange or in which the claimant has either not paid himself or colluded with the defaulter in evasion of margin payable on bargains in any security; (b) [deleted] (c) which arises from any arrangement for settlement of claims in lieu of bona fide money payment in full on the day when such claims become due; (d) which is in respect of a loan with or without security; (e) which is not filed with the Defaulters'

Committee within such time of date of declaration of default as maybe prescribed by the relevant authority. Claims against Defaulting Representative trading member (25) The Defaulters' Committee shall entertain the claim of a trading member against a defaulter in respect of loss incurred by it by reason of the failure of the constituents introduced by such defaulter to fulfill their obligations arising out of dealings which are permitted on the Exchange and made subject to the Bye Laws, Rules and Regulations of the Exchange provided the defaulter was duly registered as a representative trading member working with such creditor member. Claims of Defaulters' Committee (26) A claim of a defaulter whose estate is represented by the Defaulters' Committee against another defaulter shall not have any priority over the claims of other creditor members but shall rank with other claims as provided in Byelaw 23 (b) above. Assignment of Claims on Defaulter's Estate (27) A trading member being a creditor of a defaulter shall not sell, assign or pledge its claim on the estate of such defaulter without the consent of the relevant authority. Proceedings in the Name of or against the defaulter (28) The Defaulters' Committee shall be empowered to (a) initiate any proceedings in a court of law either in the name of the Exchange or in the name of the defaulter against any person for the purpose of recovering any amounts due to the defaulter (b) to initiate any proceedings in a court of law either in the name of the Exchange or in the name of the creditors (who have become creditors of the defaulter as a result of transactions executed subject to Byelaws, Rules and Regulations of the Exchange) of the defaulter against the defaulter for the purpose of recovering any amounts due from the defaulter. The defaulter as well as the creditors of the defaulter shall be deemed to have appointed the Exchange as their constituted attorney for the purpose of taking such proceedings. Payment of Defaulters‘ Committee (29) If any trading member takes any proceedings in a court of law against a defaulter whether during the period of its default or subsequent to its re-admission to enforce any claim against the defaulter's estate arising out of any transaction or dealing in the market made subject to the Bye 46 Confidential Laws, Rules and Regulations of the Exchange before it was declared a defaulter and obtains a decree and recovers any sum of money thereon it shall pay such amount or any portion thereof as may be fixed by the relevant authority to the Defaulters' Committee for the benefit and on account of the creditor members having claims against such defaulter. (30) The Defaulters‘ Committee for the purpose of this Chapter shall be a Committee as may be constituted by the Board of Directors from time to time. The composition of Defaulters' Committee shall be such as maybe prescribed by SEBI. (31) Notwithstanding anything to the contrary contained in this Chapter, where any securities are lodged for rectification of company objection arising out of signature difference or otherwise against a defaulter, the Exchange or National Securities Clearing Corporation Limited (Clearing Corporation) shall, after satisfying itself about the bonafides of the receiving members/ client of the receiving member, acquire the securities in its own name for the benefit of or in trust for the receiving member/ client of the receiving member. The Exchange/ Clearing Corporation may upon payment of such charges as it may prescribe, sell or otherwise dispose of the securities so acquired or transfer the securities to the receiving member/ client of the receiving member, in full and final satisfaction of the claim; Provided that the Exchange/ Clearing Corporation shall be free to require such receiving member/ client of the receiving member to indemnify the Exchange and Clearing Corporation in such form and manner as it may prescribe, as a condition precedent; Provided further that such payment of sale proceeds or transfer of securities to the receiving member/ client of the receiving member shall discharge the claim completely and no further claim shall lie against the defaulter on any ground whatsoever. 47 Confidential CHAPTER XIII INVESTOR PROTECTION FUND (1) In respect of such market segment of the Exchange as may be prescribed by the Exchange, an Investor Protection Fund (IPF) to be held in trust by National Stock Exchange Investor Protection Fund Trust (Trust) shall be maintained to make good claims for compensation which may be submitted by a trading member's Constituent who suffers loss arising from the said trading member being declared as a defaulter by the Exchange under Chapter XII. No claim of a claimant, who is a Trading Member of the Exchange or an associate of a Trading Member, shall be eligible for compensation from the IPF unless he has acted as a Constituent of the said trading member to the extent permitted by the Exchange. (2) Subject to this Part, the amount which any claimant shall be entitled to claim as compensation shall be the amount of the actual loss suffered by him less the amount or value of all monies or other benefits received or receivable by him from any source in reduction of the loss. (3) The amount that may be paid under this Part to a claimant shall not exceed such amount as may be decided by the Trust from time to time. The Trust shall disburse the compensation to the claimants as and when claims have been crystallised against the defaulter and admitted for payment by the Trust based on the recommendations, if an y, of the Defaulters' Committee and such compensation shall not be more than the maximum amount fixed for a single claim. (4) The Trust shall have the power to utilise amounts out of the IPF, subject to maximum permissible limits for each Constituent, in cases mentioned below: (i) In cases where the Trading Member informs the Exchange of his intention to pursue arbitration against the order of the GRC in favour of the Constituent, within 7 days from the date of signing of GRC order, and the admissible claim value is not more than Rupees Twenty Lakhs, then 50% of the admissible claim value or Rs. 2.00 lakhs, whichever is less, shall be released to the Constituent from IPF of the Exchange. (ii) In case the arbitration award is in favour of the Constituent in the matter as mentioned in clause (i) above or Arbitration award in favour of the constituent is not more than Rupees Twenty Lakhs in the matter directly filed for arbitration and the Member conveys his intention of preferring appeal against such arbitral award within 7 days from the date of receipt of the award, then 50% of the award amount or Rs. 3.00 lakhs, whichever is less will be released to the constituent from IPF of the Exchange. The amount released shall exclude the amount already released to the constituent at clause (i) above. (iii) In case the appellate arbitration award is in favour of the constituent and the trading member conveys his intention of filing petition in court to set aside the Appellate arbitration award u/s 34 of the Arbitration and Conciliation Act, 1996 within 7 days from the receipt of the Appellate Arbitration Award, then 75% of the amount determined in the appellate arbitration award or Rs. 5.00 lakhs (Rs. Five Lakhs), whichever is less will be released to the Constituent from IPF of the Exchange. The amount released shall exclude the amount already released to the constituent at clause (i) and (ii) above. 48 Confidential (iv) Before release of the said amounts from the IPF to the Constituent, the Exchange shall obtain appropriate undertaking or indemnity from the Constituent against the release of the amount from IPF, to ensure return of the amount so released to the Constituent, in case the proceedings are decided against the Constituent. (v) If it is observed that there is an attempt by Constituent either individually or through collusion with Trading Member(s) or with any other stakeholders, to misuse the clauses (i) to (iv) above, then without prejudice to the powers of SEBI to take action, appropriate action in this regard shall be taken against any such person, by the Relevant Authority, including disqualification of the person so involved from henceforth accessing the benefits of these provisions. (vi) The amount released to the Constituent from IPF as per the admissible claim will be replenished back to IPF from the deposit or collaterals or any other amounts, including the blocked amount of the Trading Member available with the Exchange/NSCCL and the balance will be paid to the Constituent in the following cases: (a) The Trading Member informs the Exchange, within 7 days from the date of signing of GRC directions ascertaining the admissible claim amount, his intention to refer the matter to arbitration and fails to refer the matter to arbitration within the prescribed time limit i.e. three years. (b) The Trading Member fails to inform the Exchange his intention to prefer an appeal before Appellate Arbitrators of the Exchange or court or intention to make a request u/s 33 of Arbitration and Conciliation Act, 1996 for rectification or correction of award, against the arbitral award, within 7 days from the date of receipt of award. (c) The Trading Member informs the Exchange his intention to prefer an appeal before Appellate Arbitrators of the Exchange or court but fails to prefer the same within prescribed time limit (one month from date of receipt of award in case of appellate arbitration and three months from date of receipt of award, in case of petition in court). For cases where request is made under Section 33 of Arbitration and Conciliation Act, 1996 for clarification or rectification of award, the one month period in case of appeal and three months period in case of petition mentioned above will be from the date of receipt of the order passed by arbitrator u/s 33 applications by the Trading Member. (d) The matter is decided in favour of the constituent after conclusion of arbitration or appellate arbitration or court proceedings and the Trading Member decides not to pursue the matter further. (vii) In case Constituent loses at any stage of the proceedings and decides not to pursue the matter further, then the Constituent shall refund the amount released from IPF, back to the IPF of the Exchange. In case the Constituent fails to make good the amount released out of IPF then the Constituent (based on the PAN of the Constituent) shall not be allowed to trade on any of the Exchanges till such time the Constituent refunds the amount to IPF. Further the securities lying in the demat account(s) of the Constituent shall be frozen till such time as the Constituent refunds the amount to the IPF. 49 Confidential (viii) The Exchange may be empowered to initiate any proceedings in a court of law for the purpose of recovering any amounts due to the IPF, against such Constituent who fails to make good the amount released to him out of IPF as mentioned in clause (vii) above. (5) The Trust shall have the power to utilise corpus and interest earned on the corpus of the IPF for meeting expenses or claims relating to services provided to investors as stipulated by SEBI or Board from time to time. (6) Notwithstanding anything contained in any other Byelaw, the Trust shall have the power to utilise the interest income earned on the investments made out of IPF, either in part or whole, for educating investors, creating awareness among the investor community at large and for any research connected therewith or incidental thereto. (7) The Exchange shall publish in all editions of at least one English national daily with wide circulation and in at least one regional language daily with wide circulation, a notice specifying a date not being less than 3 months after the said publication, on or before which claims for compensation shall be made in relation to the defaulter specified in the notice. The notice shall contain the specified period, the maximum compensation limit for a single claim of a claimant, etc. The said notice shall also be displayed on the premises of the Exchange as well as on the web-site of the Exchange for the entire specified period. (8) A claim for compensation in respect of a default shall be made in writing to the Exchange on or before the date specified in the said notice and any claim which is not so made shall be barred unless the Trust otherwise determines. The Exchange shall process the claims in accordance with procedures as may be laid down by Defaulters' Committee and if the assets of the defaulter are insufficient to meet the approved claims, it shall forward the claims along with the recommendations of the Defaulters' Committee to the Trust. However, the Trust need not wait for the realization of the assets of the defaulter before the disbursement towards claims. (9) A claimant under this Chapter must sign an undertaking to be bound by the decision of the Trust whose decision shall be final and binding. (10) The Trust in disallowing (whether wholly or partly) a claim for compensation shall serve notice of such disallowance on the claimant. (11) The Trust, if satisfied that the default on which the claim is founded was actually committed, may allow the claim and act accordingly. (12) The Trust may at any time and from time to time require the claimant to produce and deliver any securities, documents or statements of evidence necessary to support any claim made or necessary for the purpose of establishing his claims and in default of delivery of any such securities, documents or statements of evidence by such claimant, the Trust may disallow any claim by him under this Chapter. (13) Contributions shall be made to the IPF from the following sources:- (a) 1 % of the listing fees received, on a quarterly basis (b) 100 % of the interest earned on the 1 % security deposit kept by the issuer companies at the time of the offering of securities for subscription to the public, immediately on refund of the deposit 50 Confidential (c) The difference of amount of auctions / close out price (d) The amount received from the proceeds of the sale of the securities written off as per para 4 & 5 of SEBI circular No. FITTC/FII/02/2002 dated May15, 2002 (e) The amounts specified in pursuance of Regulation 28 (12) (e) (ii), Regulation 28 (13) and Regulation 29(2) of SEBI (Substantial Acquisition of Shares and Takeovers) Regulations 1997. (f) Such contribution by trading members of the Exchange as may be decided by the Exchange from time to time based on the transaction value. The Exchange shall further be empowered to call for such additional contributions as may be required from time to time to make up for the shortfall, if any, in the IPF, at the discretion of theExchange. (14) The IPF to be held in trust as aforesaid shall vest with the Trust which shall administer the same. The IPF shall be well segregated and shall be immune from any liabilities of the Exchange. (15) The Exchange, in consultation with the Trust, shall review and progressively increase the amount of compensation available against a single claim from an investor every three years. The Exchange shall disseminate the compensation limit fixed and any change thereof, to the public through a Press Release and also through web site of the Exchange. (16) The Trust may seek the advice of the Defaulters' Committee as to the eligibility or otherwise of individual claims of investors. (17) The Exchange shall arrange to provide administrative assistance to the Trust to facilitate the processing and settlement of investor claims. (18) The claims of the claimants arising out of speculative transactions or which are sham or collusive shall not be eligible for compensation from the IPF. (19) The balance of the IPF lying unutilised with the Trust shall continue to be utilised only for such purposes as prescribed by SEBI. In the event of winding up of the Exchange, the balance lying unutilised with the Trust shall be transferred to SEBI. The funds will be maintained in a separate account and SEBI would act as Trustee of these funds to be utilised for purposes of investor education, awareness and research. (20) Investor Service Fund The Exchange shall set up an Investor Services Fund in accordance with the terms and conditions prescribed by SEBI from time to time. 51 Confidential CHAPTER XIV MISCELLANEOUS (1) The relevant authority shall be empowered to impose such restrictions on transactions in one or more Exchange securities as the relevant authority in its judgment deems advisable in the interest of maintaining a fair and orderly market in the securities or if it otherwise deems advisable in the public interest or for the protection of investors. During the effectiveness of such restrictions, no trading member shall, for any account in which it has an interest or for the account of any client, engage in any transaction in contravention of such restrictions. (2) Any failure to observe or comply with any requirement of this Bye Law, or any Bye Laws, Rules or Regulations, where applicable, may be dealt with by the relevant authority as a violation of such Bye Laws, Rules or Regulations. (3) Trading members have an obligation as the trading members of the Exchange to inform the relevant authority of the Exchange and the Securities Exchange Board of India about insider trading, information on takeover and other such information/ practices as may be construed as being detrimental to the efficient operations of the Exchange and as may be required under SEBI Act and Rules and Regulations. (4) Save as otherwise specifically provided in the regulations prescribed by the relevant authority regarding clearing and settlement arrangement, in promoting, facilitating, assisting, regulating, managing and operating the Exchange, the Exchange should not be deemed to have incurred any liability, and accordingly no claim or recourse, in respect of, in relation to, any dealing in securities or any matter connected therewith shall lie against the Exchange or any authorised person(s) acting for the Exchange. (5) No claim, suit, prosecution or other legal proceedings shall lie against the Exchange or any authorised person(s) acting for the Exchange, in respect of anything which is in good faith done or intended to be done in pursuance of any order or other binding directive issued to the Exchange under any law or delegated legislation for the time being in force.

www.ingramcontent.com/pod-product-compliance
Ingram Content Group UK Ltd.
Pitfield, Milton Keynes, MK11 3LW, UK
UKHW040009200726
13854UKWH00001B/117